# Christian Ethics
# for Today:

An Evangelical Approach

# Christian Ethics for Today:

## An Evangelical Approach

**Milton L. Rudnick**

**BAKER BOOK HOUSE**
**Grand Rapids, Michigan**

TO ROB

# CONTENTS

# PREFACE

For more than a decade I have been teaching ethics to college students, and have searched in vain for a suitable textbook. There are, of course, a number of works which discuss ethics from an evangelical perspective. For various reasons, however, they have not worked well for me and my classes. Some have been too challenging, technical, or sophisticated to serve as an introductory text for college students. They have assumed a degree of theological and philosophical expertise not often found in undergraduates. Others have seemed superficial or simplistic, and this is just as much a problem as the opposite extreme.

Ethics is a demanding, complicated, and ambiguous field of study. It deals with some deep, dark, and very sticky questions. To be helpful to students, a textbook must be both comprehensible and sufficiently comprehensive to enable them to cope with the issues and problems which they confront. One of my goals in preparing this book has been to meet these criteria.

Another consideration which is very important is theological adequacy, for Christian ethics is a theological discipline. Although it is also related to philosophy, the relation to theology is closer and stronger, at least in a Christian academic community. To be theologically adequate, in my judgment, an ethical approach must be consistent and compatible with one's theological orientation. More than that, the ethical approach must grow out of the very heart and center of his theology. This explains another kind of difficulty that I experienced with some textbooks on Christian ethics. The theological orientation and even the theological substance diverged from my own to the point that their usefulness was seriously impaired.

My own theological orientation is a supreme commitment to the gospel of Jesus Christ, both as the object of faith and as the central and integrating theme of the Christian message, and to Scripture as God's own inspired and infallible witness to that gospel. It is from this perspective that I think and write in ethics as well as in theology. I hope that others who share this perspective will find this book useful. I also hope that some whose convictions and orientation are decidedly different from mine will find this to be a clear and meaningful statement of that with which they take issue. My own experience in the formal study of ethics reveals that few who teach and write in this field work from the approach which I employ here.

In the jargon of ethicists, I am a rules-deontologist with a contextualist bent. Most teachers and authors in the field of Christian ethics (and, consequently, most students) are committed to some form of teleological or contextualist ethics. Those committed to teleological ethics determine right and wrong primarily from anticipated results, while those adhering to contextualist ethics determine right and wrong by analysis of the context, by attempting to discern what God is doing or what He wills in a given context. The Christian rules-deontologist, while attentive to future results and the present context, seeks direction primarily from divinely revealed and universally binding principles of conduct. Since so few rules-deontologists are writing these days, some teleologists and contextualists may appreciate a fresh expression of this position for purposes of comparison and discussion.

I would like to express gratitude to the hundreds of students who, over the years, have participated with me in the study of Christian ethics, and who, in some cases, have consulted with me about their personal ethical decisions. They have provided much intellectual and professional stimulation as well as a testing ground for this material. In addition, I owe thanks to James B. Nelson and Wilson Yates of United Theological Seminary, New Brighton, Minnesota, with whom I have recently studied. Although their theological and ethical orientations are different from mine (and from one another's) they have helped me with the basic skills of ethical reflection and have offered valuable criticism. My wife, children, friends, and colleagues have been a source of deep personal encouragement. I am grateful to all.

Milton L. Rudnick
St. Paul, Minnesota

# INTRODUCTION

## I. DEFINITIONS

The serious discussion of almost any subject requires a definition of terms. This is especially true when the subject is ethics. How would you define the term *ethics?* What images, concepts, or actions does this word evoke in your mind? What mood or overtones do you associate with it? How does "ethics" compare with "morals" or "morality"? In what ways are they alike? In what ways are they different?

On the one hand, most people have a general impression of what ethics is about. They know that right and wrong are associated with it, perhaps also rules and standards of conduct. Conscience seems to belong in there somewhere. However, without a considerable amount of previous thought and experience, not many can produce a sufficiently complete and precise definition. It is especially difficult to distinguish between ethics and morals. They are often used synonymously, even by the experts. And yet, somehow, they have a different ring and feel. How shall we denote this difference?

Any definition of terms tends to be somewhat arbitrary. Ultimately words mean, for us, what we want them to mean, and their meanings may vary from situation to situation. The word *screw*, for example, may mean "to fasten with a threaded metal pin," or "to cheat," or "to make a mistake," or "to engage in the sex act." So, to define a term is more a descriptive task than a prescriptive one. A definition tells how a term is used, and what it means, in a given frame of reference. It does not attempt to say how it must be used or what it means in all situations. The definitions given below explain the way several key terms are used in this book. They are offered, by way of introduction, to focus the reader's thoughts.

## A. Ethics Is Theory

*Ethics*, as the term is used here, is theory. It is an intellectual exercise, a process of reflection, analysis, decision, and evaluation. The purpose of the ethical enterprise is to decide what is right and wrong to do. Its primary concern is proper conduct, but it also gives consideration to the attitudes and motives from which conduct issues. In order to do ethics, as it is perceived in this book, one must have an adequate set of principles, guidelines, directives, and a workable process by which the principles are applied to the problems and issues which he confronts. Ethics, understood in this way, happens in the head as well as in the heart. It involves thought and judgment as well as commitment.

## B. Evangelical Ethics

An evangelical approach to ethics is a method of determining right and wrong which grows out of a particular understanding and interpretation of the Christian message. Evangelical ethics is, first of all, Christian ethics. Of course, it is possible to develop workable ethics from the assumptions and beliefs of other Christian perspectives, and from non-Christian religions. It is even possible to develop ethics without relation to any religious point of view. Much, in fact, most ethics is built on philosophical rather than religious foundations. However, here we present an approach which is religious rather than philosophical; Christian rather than non-Christian; and evangelical rather than liberal, neo-orthodox, or Roman Catholic, for example.

### 1. Christocentricity

In order for ethics to be evangelical, it must reflect the basic emphases of evangelical Christians. First of all, it must be Christocentric. That is to say, evangelical ethics must keep Christ and His redemptive work in the center of the discussion. Christ must be regarded, not only as the source of forgiveness and eternal life, but also as the source of ethical guidance and the source of the power to change. To put it in traditional theological language, not only justification but also sanctification must be recognized as the gift and work of His grace.

A vital aspect of Christocentricity as evangelicals perceive it is the distinction between law and gospel. For our ethical reflection to be valid we must carefully observe the difference between what God demands and what He gives, as well as the relations between them. Similarly, we must be aware of the differences between them. Evangelicals are by no means the only Christians who are committed to Christocentricity and the law-gospel dichotomy. However, these emphases are more prominent among them than among others.

### 2. Scripture-based

The other basic emphasis that should characterize evangelical ethics is a very high view of biblical authority. The gospel of Jesus Christ is the heart of the message as well as its unifying element. Scripture is its source, the divinely inspired record of God's atoning love for us in Jesus Christ. It is also the revelation of His will for us. To understand what we should do or avoid in life, as well as to know what we should believe, we consult the Bible. Evangelical ethics as well as evangelical theology should be based solidly on Scripture. The Bible is the only source and norm of Christian teaching and practice.

### 3. Diversity

The approach to ethics developed in this book seriously attempts to reflect these emphases. To the extent that it succeeds it can properly be called "an evangelical approach to ethics." It is *an* evangelical approach, not *the* evangelical approach to ethics. There is no single, definitive treatment of evangelical ethics, and not all evangelical ethicists agree with one another. There is, in fact, wide diversity among evangelicals, for various reasons. Individual human uniqueness accounts for some of the diversity. No two human beings perceive, understand, or explain anything in precisely the same ways. And certainly, denominational differences cause some of the varying perspectives.

Furthermore, the data is less complete in ethics than in the other theological disciplines. To a large extent ethics deals with questions and problems about which we have no explicit, unambiguous biblical testimony. This means that in doing the work of ethics we must operate with inference and human opinion and judgment more extensively than in the other disciplines. People are inclined to disagree even more about their opinions and judgments than they are about what Scripture says and means.

Then, too, not all ethicists hold to the same view of Scripture. Some regard all of Scripture as God's inspired and binding revelation (the position assumed in this book). Others feel that the authenticity and divine authority of a given passage must be established by historical-critical analysis.

Finally, the basic approach of evangelical ethicists may vary. This book takes what is called a rules-deontological approach, an approach that says we must determine right and wrong by means of divinely given ethical directives. Other ethicists, including some evangelicals, take a teleological approach, which determines right and wrong on the basis of expected results. Still others are contextualists, who attempt to determine right and wrong largely, if not exclusively, by analysis of the context.

To complicate the picture still further, we must admit that even ethicists of the same confessional commitment, using the same basic approach, and operating with the same view of Scripture do not always come to the same conclusions.

### 4. *Maintaining perspective*

I point out this diversity in the interest of maintaining a proper perspective. In this book I present directly and unequivocally the approach which to me best seems to express what Scripture and evangelical theology teach about knowing and doing what is right. Then I plug these elements into a problem-solving process which facilitates their application to daily life. Although I try to indicate the difference between my judgments and God's revealed truth, this may not always be as clear as it should be. Furthermore, I make no claim to infallibility. As with the theological and ethical work of any individual, this material should be tested against Scripture for accuracy and adequacy. It is certain that some ethicists, especially those from different backgrounds, operating with different assumptions and methods, will take issue with much that I have written.

### C. Morality Is Practice

We must define two other basic terms: *morals* and *morality*. These terms refer to practice, the practical application of ethical decisions to daily life. The distinction between ethics and morality is the difference between theory and practice, or the difference between deciding and doing. By means of ethical reflection and analysis I come to a conclusion about what I should or should not do. My morality or immorality is revealed in the extent to which I live by that conclusion.

Good morals do not always follow good ethics. Theory is not always put into practice. A person may be brilliant, and skilled and sensitive in ethical reasoning, and yet may act immorally. To know the good is not necessarily to do it. On the other hand, a person may be inept at ethical reflection and inarticulate in ethical discussion, and yet lead an obedient Christian life—he might be a poor ethicist but a moral person. Morality happens in the life and conduct, while ethics, as we mentioned, happens in the head and heart.

## II. TRENDS

Like everything human, Christian ethics is in movement. To get a sense of where we are currently in the area of Christian ethics it is important to realize where we have been as well as observe the direction in which we seem to be headed.

### A. The Fact of Ethical Change

Ideas of what is right and wrong, at least about some things, change from generation to generation. This is true not only of society in general, but of Christians in particular, even Christians of the same confessional commitment, and even of Christians who cherish their tradition and encourage conformity to it. Indeed, when members of a later generation use the same ethical approach as their forefathers, they may come to different conclusions. In some cases these changes appear to be for the better, but in others they may seem to be for the worse.

When I was younger there was a large consensus (although it was not unanimous) among evangelical clergy that contraception was morally wrong. Few clergy today agree with those views and judgments. What brought about the change? What is the nature of the change? Is it moral laxity, decline of standards, lack of earnestness, accommodation to worldly values? Not necessarily. To some extent, at least, change may be the result of a better understanding of the issues and a more careful interpretation of Scripture.

In some cases moral standards have become more rigorous. For example, previous generations of clergy and laity were largely tolerant of racism. Racist remarks and discriminatory policies were prevalent in evangelical churches and few regarded this as wrong. While much room for improvement remains, today consciences are much more sensitive to the evils of racism, and racist policies in many evangelical congregations and schools have been rescinded. Certainly part of the impetus for change was pressure from society. However, anyone who has lived through the transition can testify to the impact of biblical and ethical study.

The fact of ethical change is undeniable. It is inevitable and, in many cases, desirable. Times and circumstances change. The significance of things may change. New light may be shed both on moral issues and on the meaning of Scripture passages which speak to the issues. While Christians must be on guard against moral laxity and erosion of moral values, they must not resist and reject all ethical change.

## B. The Current Ethical Revolution

However, the "new morality" that we have been experiencing since the 1960s is not this type of natural and necessary updating of ethical views on the basis of new information. It is more than a revision of some ethical conclusions. It is, in fact, an ethical revolution in which the principles of Christian ethics have been assaulted and repudiated by many. In fact, the basic process by which Christians for centuries have arrived at ethical decisions has been replaced by radically different approaches.

The problem is not simply that people are sinning more and obeying less. The problem is, rather, that a growing number of people in the world, as well as in Christian circles, refuse to consider many types of behavior as sin. These people insist on approving certain activities and attitudes though they are clearly identified as sin in Scripture. Homosexuality, self-assertion, and revolution are some examples. Conversely, virtues and values commended by Scripture, such as chastity, non-retaliation, and self-sacrifice, are scorned by some of the same people. What we are confronted with is not merely deviation from Christian moral standards but a wholesale rejection of these standards, and, in some cases, the rejection of the notion that revealed, enduring, binding moral standards exist.

The result is a radical ethical relativism bordering on anarchy. Each person feels free to decide for himself what is good and what is evil. Right and wrong are reduced to personal preference or opinion. "If you enjoy it, it is good," many would say. Others with more social sensitivity might put it this way: "If most people in a given situation enjoy it or benefit from it, it is good." In all fairness it must be said that few Christian ethicists, even those who question the concept of divinely revealed ethical norms, come out in favor of this kind of pleasure-centered and self-centered approach. However, without intending to, they appear to be encouraging it. To deny that God has given us clear and binding ethical guidelines is to invite ethical confusion and revolt.

## C. The Counterrevolution

The revolution in ethical theory and moral practice has not gone unchallenged. It has, in fact, provoked something of a counterrevolution. At both the scholarly and popular levels critics have taken issue with the theoretical basis as well as the practical consequences of the new morality. Pastors have preached against it; teachers have taught against it; authors have written against it. Furthermore, the polemic against the new morality has been combined with a reaffirmation and defense of conventional Christian ethics and morality.

The resurgence of conservative religious movements with

strict moral codes may be, in part, a reaction against the ethical revolution. Political movements of the far right with their law-and-order emphasis may also represent such a reaction. The phenomenon of Bill Gothard's Basic Youth Conflicts Seminars is clearly a counterrevolutionary measure. In these meetings large crowds gather to listen to long lectures by Gothard in which he spells out a very extensive, specific, and conservative moral code he claims is derived from the Bible. In his presentations Rev. Gothard describes his program as a campaign to turn America back to conservative religion and morality. The large and appreciative response he receives reveals the alarm and disenchantment many feel regarding the new morality.

### D. The Search for Direction

Confused and frightened by a rapidly changing world, the collapse of traditional values and institutions, the overwhelming possibilities of the new technologies, and conflicts in self, families, and society, many people want to know what they ought to do. They sense that they need help in trying to decide what is right and what is wrong. Those who are Christians quite naturally look to their churches and spiritual leaders. However, they may not be receiving all the help that they desire or need.

In my judgment, many evangelical pastors and educators are not well prepared for ethical leadership roles. The situation is improving; however, too often in professional curricula, courses in Christian ethics have been electives. Although we expect our pastors and educators to lead good Christian lives, and although we also expect them to help others do the same, we have not always provided them with the knowledge and skills which facilitate this. Because sanctification in the Christian is the work of the Holy Spirit, we apparently assume that it will happen without the disciplined reflection that ethics involves. Some still actually express suspicion of and contempt for the formal study of ethics. Who needs it? Doesn't a sense of right and wrong come "naturally" to a Christian? Or, can't we resolve all of our ethical dilemmas by the Golden Rule? Isn't ethics legalistic?

This book was written out of the conviction that ethics can be evangelical and that evangelicals ought to be more concerned about ethics. It is designed to assist those who are seeking ethical direction themselves and who, in some cases, wish to prepare themselves for ethical leadership roles. Many of my students are studying to be pastors, teachers, and directors of Christian education. Others, whose vocational goals are outside the professional service of the church, simply wish to equip themselves spiritually and intellectually to make responsible, valid, and God-pleasing life decisions. My hope is that this material will be helpful to those who are seeking direction.

### E. Answers or Questions?

Despite my commitment to the deontological (rule-based) approach, I do not view ethics so much as a set of answers, but as a way of asking questions. Rather than attempt to provide readers with solutions to all or even some of of their ethical and moral problems, my goal is to present a process of inquiry by which they can arrive at their own solutions. My views and conclusions on certain issues will become evident, but only by way of illustration, to indicate how the process works. Ultimately, we must all make our own ethical decisions.

*moral disability*
*and ethical confusion*

# 1 CORRUPTION

What is wrong with human beings, anyway? Why is it so difficult for us to do the right thing? Why is it so difficult even to know what is right? Why is there so much conflict within and among us? No realistic consideration of ethics can go very far without facing up to these painful and discouraging questions.

The Christian diagnosis of the root cause of this unpromising human condition is: sin. Those who turn to Christianity for meaning and hope hear, first of all, some very bad news. Man's ethical and moral problem is not a minor one. It is extremely serious. The reason for our moral disability and ethical confusion is that we are possessed and ruined by an evil power. The hold of evil upon us is pervasive, profound, and the consequences are disastrous. We are thoroughly and, as far as all human resources are concerned, hopelessly corrupt.

It is important to note that sin, as Scripture describes it, is the ruination of the good. Evil has no independent existence. In this respect the Christian understanding of evil is different from other philosophies and religions which teach that a dark and evil force has always existed and worked against the good power of God. Scripture, on the other hand, teaches that God alone in His goodness has existed from all eternity, and that evil has emerged and spread within the good creation that He made.

The details of the origin of evil are shrouded in mystery. However, the nature of evil as the distortion of that which was good is clearly revealed. Everything evil is something good gone out of control. Pride, for example, is self-respect enlarged disproportionately. Lust is the sexual impulse running unchecked or misdirected. Greed is an appreciation for material things which has become idolatrous or selfish. Every vice is a virtue turned upside down or inside out. Everything evil is something good that has been corrupted. The source and mastermind of all evil is a fallen angel.

## I. GOD'S CREATURES

Behind this interpretation of evil as the corrupted good is faith in God as the Creator. We human beings and everything else in the universe have been made by Him. However, He is not responsible for what is wrong with us. He is not the source or cause of the corruption that mars and threatens us. He is only the source of what is right with and about us.

### A. Created Good

Not only Adam and Eve but all human beings, including you, were created good. That information may come as a surprise. We are accustomed to hearing only (and this will be stated on pp. 26 f.) that we have been sinful from the very beginning of our existence. However, it is also true that each of us was created good.

In this connection it is important to keep in mind that God's work of creation in you is a continuous process. It is not something that happens only once, at conception or birth; it goes on throughout life as God develops and sustains you. Not only physically, but also psychologically, emotionally, intellectually, and in every other way God is supporting you and unfolding you as a person.

Furthermore, you are a unique product of His creative art. No one else in human history has ever been exactly like you in appearance, personality, or ability, and no future individual will be an exact replica. Like everything else that He does, God's creative work in you is good—perfect, in fact. God makes no blunders when He creates. There are no unfortunate omissions or defects in His creation. As the young black child quoted in Transactional Analysis literature says, "God don't make no junk!"

## B. Created for Fellowship

God had a definite purpose in mind when He created man, an exciting and ennobling purpose not shared by any other earth creature. His purpose was and is that human beings might be aware of Him, that we might know who He is and what He is like. He created us with a capacity for fellowship with Him, that we might be close to Him in a bond of love, trust, and respect. This, of course, involves the ability to communicate with Him—we have senses to perceive His revelation, minds to assimilate it, hearts to believe, as well as means of responding to Him in attitude, word, and deed.

God made us to be in intimate and constant contact with Him, listening and answering, receiving and giving. Other creatures on this planet were made for the environment and for each other. We human beings, in addition, were made for God Himself, for a conscious and loving relationship with Him. Until and unless that fellowship is established we are missing the very purpose of our existence and will experience frustration and emptiness as a result. As Augustine says, "Thou hast formed us for Thyself, and our hearts are restless till they find their rest in Thee."

## C. Created in God's Image

Through a close relationship with us God desires to exert an influence on us. Through our awareness of Him and interaction with Him He wants us to become like Him, to acquire His own attitudes and ways. Actually, something like this happens in all close personal relationships. Every human being to whom you have been close has left an impression on you. Consciously or unconsciously you adopt some values, mannerisms, and behavior patterns of the people who are important to you. After years of living together, especially if the relationship is warm and close, a husband and wife will often begin to physically resemble one another.

In a very real and profound way God is working to make us like Himself. He made us in His own image, the Bible says. In this case, since God is not a physical being, the resemblance implied in this word *image* is not physical. Rather it is a *moral* likeness. God made us to be like Him in character and conduct. What, in a word, sums up God's character and conduct? "God is love" (I John 4:8).

Through a close personal relationship in which He lavishes the fullness of His love upon us, God intends to stimulate and cultivate in us the kind of love that characterizes Him. "No man has ever seen God; if we love one another, God abides in us and his love is perfected in us" (I John 4:12, RSV). The invisible God becomes "visible" in the loving actions of those who are in fellowship with Him. We are to become the physical human manifestations, projections, and replicas of the God who relates to us in love.

## II. CORRUPT FROM BIRTH

Paradoxically, despite God's good creative work in us and despite His high purpose and destiny for us, we are not born good, free, and pure. Rather, we are born corrupt, sinful, enslaved by evil. We are born losers—all of us.

### A. Corruption Simultaneous with Creation

The relationship between God's good creation in us and our corruption by sin is not what we might expect. It is not that we were first created good and then subsequently corrupted. It is not that by conception, prenatal development, and birth God produced an innocent child who then was tempted and defiled by exposure to the evil influences of the world.

Rather, from the very beginning of our existence, and throughout life as the process of creation continues, we are constantly being corrupted by sin. As God proceeds with our origin and development He performs each step perfectly. And yet, at each step Satan intervenes to distort, pervert, wreck what God has done. The devil cannot create anyone or anything, for only God can create. However, the devil can corrupt, and he does this in each of us from the very beginning of the creative process and keeps on doing so as long as we are alive.

By way of illustration imagine an automobile manufacturing plant in which every part was perfect and all assembly work was done correctly. The result should have been absolutely perfect automobiles. However, at each step of the process, as these perfect parts were being perfectly assembled, a saboteur wrecked what was done—marred the polished surfaces of the moving parts, put foreign and abrasive materials into fuel and lubricants, shorted-out the electrical system, disrupted vital linkages, disturbed delicate adjustments—with the result that the finished product, though perfectly made, was, nevertheless, junk.

Our corruption by sin occurs simultaneously with our creation by God. Our human nature is, on the one hand, God's good creation. On the other hand, it is also thoroughly and completely corrupt. From a human point of view it is nearly impossible to tell the difference between God's creation in us and our corruption. However, Scripture carefully distinguishes between them, and it is important for us also to be aware of the difference. One who does not realize the difference might regard God as the source of sinfulness. He might reason incorrectly that since we are sinful from the very beginning of our existence and since God is our Creator, God must also be the Creator of sin. This would be a serious and dangerous error. The differences between creation and corruption is the difference between God's work and that of the devil.

## B. Corruption As Deficiency

What kind of damage has the devil done to each of us? One aspect of this damage may be described as a deficiency, the lack of certain basic and vital human responses. The devil's corrupting influence, first of all, destroys our ability to respond and relate to God. The components of faith are missing, and there is no way that we ourselves can replace them. Corrupt as we are from birth we cannot respect God as we should (fear). Nor can we desire and serve God as we should (love). Nor can we confide in and rely on Him as we should (trust). Our entire attitude toward God is deficient. We are out of touch with Him from birth and unable to reestablish contact.

Our ability to respond to other people is also gravely impaired. Instead of the warm and generous attitude that is necessary for solid human realtionships, we are dominated by self-interest. It is difficult for us to love others and give of ourselves to others, unless, of course, it promises to be to our ultimate advantage. We lack the ability fully to love others just as truly as we lack the ability to believe in God.

### C.  Corruption As Evil Inclination

Corruption is more than the absence of something good and necessary. It is also the presence of something evil and destructive. The corruption of sin manifests itself in revolt against God and lovelessness toward people. We sinful human beings are driven creatures. Not only are we helpless to do the right, as was mentioned in the previous section, but we are also pushed relentlessly and manipulated constantly to do what is wrong.

Under the sway of corruption we have the uncontrollable impulse to turn against God, revolt against His will, disrespect and disobey Him. We are also strongly inclined to neglect, exploit, or hurt other people. All human conflicts are expressions of this inborn tendency toward evil, this powerful inclination to turn against God and against people. Conflicts occur when either or both parties are acting out their corruptness.

### D.  Transmission of Corruption

The corruption of sin is transmitted from parents to children. Along with a variety of traits and potentials, along with the gift of life itself, your parents conveyed to you the terrible problem of sin. The corrupting presence and power of the devil came to you through them. Automatically and inescapably from the very beginning of your existence you lacked faith and love and were inclined, instead, toward evil. This is what the term *original sin* refers to.

Many have the impression that original sin is primarily inherited guilt. They think that God blames us for the wrong done by our ancestors all the way back to Adam and Eve. It is true that there is guilt attached to original sin. However, the guilt is not for what someone else has done. Rather the guilt is related to this corruption that has been present in us from the very beginning of our existence. The newborn infant is guilty before God and under His wrath, not because he or she has done something wrong, not because he or she is being held responsible for someone else's wrong, but because he or she is corrupt.

### E. Source and Force of Corruption

The Bible reveals that the source and force of human corruption is a personal being who is intelligent, powerful, and evil. Corruption is not an accident; it is a conspiracy masterminded and implemented by Satan, God's great enemy. There are those even in Christian circles who deny that there is such a being as the devil. According to them the devil is simply an ancient mythological way of trying to account for human weakness and sin. However, the teaching of Scripture as well as a great deal of human experience confirms the reality of the devil and his role in our corruption. The devil himself may well be the one who prompts disbelief in his existence. If so, it is a very shrewd strategy. If we do not believe that he exists, we will be inclined to relax our defenses and thus be all the more vulnerable to his attacks.

### F. Corrupting Influences

The corruption which the devil initiates and perpetuates is also reinforced by the evil influences of other corrupt persons, individually and collectively. We sinful human beings have a way of bringing out the worst in one another. Corruption is spread and deepened as we treat one another lovelessly and as we are exposed to one another's irreverence, godlessness, and immorality.

Much in our culture sneers at God and His will for our lives. A great deal of what is communicated by the mass media and some of what passes for education is an attack against Christain faith and morality. All of this feeds the corruption which is already present and active in all of us. Unfortunately, even those whom we love and admire have this effect upon us at times, and we on them. The most devout, committed, wise, learned, obedient, and moral Christian you know sometimes displays and acts out his corruption and, therefore, can be an evil influence.


## III. COMPLETELY AND HOPELESSLY CORRUPT

Having considered what corruption is and how it is transmitted and strengthened, we now reflect on the extent of the problem. How much are we affected by our corruption? What can we ourselves do about it? What are the consequences?


### A. Completely Corrupt

Corruption is pervasive. It permeates every aspect of our being—body, mind, and soul. No part of us, not even our innermost being, remains untouched and uncontaminated. Our physical appetites for food, drink, rest, and sex are all ruined and twisted by sin, so that what is intrinsically good and natural takes an evil form or direction. Similarly, our minds and thoughts are corrupted, so that the faculty which was designed to enable us to know and relate to God functions, instead, to shut God out or question His very existence. Our feelings and desires which are meant to enhance and express our relationship to God and others become largely oriented toward self-satisfaction. Even our religious impulses are perverted, so that instead of recognizing and responding to the true God we are inclined to make idols of one kind or another.

Everything that we are, and also everything that we do, is affected by sin. Some of our behavior is obviously corrupt and evil. It violates either our relationship with God or our relationship with other people, or both. It is clearly contrary to God's revealed will. We may be acutely aware of the corrupt character of this behavior. However, this is only the tip of the iceberg. The sad truth is that even conduct which appears good and wholesome is tainted and unacceptable to God. Our best performance, our most obedient acts, our most sincere expressions of faith, our most generous gifts, are also marred and disqualified by our corruption.

First of all, our motives are always mixed. Even if we do something primarily out of love for God and others, there will always be some sinful selfishness present in the motive, and that spoils it. Furthermore, because of our sinfulness, our performance is never perfect, and perfection is what God requires. Consequently, everything that we do is ultimately judged by God to be inadequate and even offensive.

## B. Civil Righteousness

However, even corrupt and condemned human beings are capable of external decency, and this is very important to human survival. It would be impossible for us to live in society unless most people, most of the time, were capable of a measure of honesty, justice, generosity, and compassion. Some people who do not have faith in Christ display these and other virtues. God Himself provides them with this capability.

A residual sense of God's will remains in fallen human beings. Frequently, this is called a "natural knowledge of the law," an intuitive (though imperfect) sense of right and wrong. Some men possess the rational realization that their own well-being and that of society require the exercise of these virtues. In other words, they have the conviction that it pays to do what is right. Other men may be motivated to act in a decent and respectable manner for the emotional satisfaction that this brings.

God wills and enables this civil righteousness, as it is called, for the *temporal* welfare of people. However, it has no significance for their *eternal* welfare. It does not make them right with God or eligible for salvation. Everything done by the person who is apart from God (the unbelieving and, thus, unforgiven person)—even good conduct—is sin. Only the person who is right with God can please Him.

## C. Hopelessly Corrupt

There is no way for a human being of himself to overcome this corruption. We are hopelessly trapped, and we are not able to rescue ourselves or even significantly improve ourselves or our position. Like a person caught in quicksand, the more we struggle to save ourselves, the deeper we sink into corruption. Almost every sensitive and realistic person is aware of his own weakness and imperfection. However, that we are hopelessly corrupt is by no means self-evident. The fact is that our condition, our problem, is far worse than we could ever discover on our own.

## D.  Consequences of Corruption

God is not tolerant of corruption. He reacts against it in a radical and decisive manner. He condemns corrupt and rebellious human beings, and consigns them to everlasting punishment in hell hereafter. God does not want us to be ignorant of these consequences. In His Word, spoken and written, He exposes our corruption and warns us of the consequences. That element of His message is called "the law." By telling us what He requires and expects—and His expectations are staggering—God makes us aware of the extent to which we deviate and fail. This, in turn, is indicative of the inner corruption which is the root of all our moral problems.

It is not pleasant to learn about our corruption and its consequences. It is, in fact, very bad news. Nothing less can prepare us for the Good News of the gospel, the message of God's mercy in Christ which provides both pardon and deliverance from the consequences of corruption. Unless we know the frightening diagnosis, we will not be interested in the remedy which God provides.

## E.  Corruption in the Christian

Although forgiven and counteracted, corruption is present and active in the Christian. For the sake of Jesus, because of His sacrifice, God pardons those who trust in Him. Furthermore, through the power of the Holy Spirit He works within the Christian against the power of evil. However, although pardoned and opposed, corruption remains as a continuing threat and hindrance, even to the strongest Christian. Like diabetes, when recognized and treated, corruption can be controlled and its debilitating effects minimized. However, in this life there is no cure.

Corruption is not someone else's problem. It is your problem and mine—a problem we must face up to continually, a problem with which we must live—and die. The solution is not merely a matter of acquiring some better information, or correcting some bad habits, or gaining some new attitudes by inspiration and experience. Rather, as we have seen, the problem is deep and complex, and requires a radical solution amounting to liberation from slavery or even resurrection from the dead.

# 2 MOTIVATION

Human corruption as described in chapter 1 is depressing, frightening, immobilizing. Powerful motivation is required for us to act despite it and in the face of it. That motivation for the Christian is the gift and work of God. He moves us, for we cannot move ourselves. This is a basic part of the Good News of the gospel: the God who forgives us for the sake of Jesus Christ also enables and moves us to become new, better people.

## I. GOD OVERCOMES CORRUPTION IN JESUS CHRIST

In order to move us, God did something about the spiritual and moral corruption which traps and ruins us. He solved the great problem of sin which we could never solve. He released us from bondage to the worst elements of ourselves. He raised us from the spiritual death which had come upon us as a result of sin. Jesus is God at work in our world and in our lives, combatting the corruption of sin, rescuing and restoring the victims of corruption.

*35*

## A. Jesus Reveals Our Potential

Jesus provides us with a vision of uncorrupted humanity. He is a living, moving example of what we are supposed to be and can be with His help. He is the only whole and completely authentic human being who has ever lived. The more fully we are made aware of His human personality and life, the better we know our own potential. A model is an essential and a very powerful motivating factor. Most often we look only to other sinful human beings as models. Although some may exemplify Christian values and conduct, all are limited and hindered by their sinfulness.

Unfortunately, most of our fellow human beings—even our fellow Christians—do not serve as good models at all. As was observed in chapter 1, we tend to drag down and disillusion one another because we are so often acting out our corruption rather than the love and will of God. All of this underscores the importance of Jesus' matchless and flawless human life and personality as a motivating factor. He came, in part, to show us what we ourselves can become.

That a model can be motivating is clear from much human experience. Educators in ghetto schools have discovered that students' eyes are opened and their sights are elevated significantly by contact with prominent and successful persons of their own ethnic or racial background.

Patients in amputee wards of military hospitals after World War II, many of whom had given up hope of resuming a normal life, were startled by the strange behavior of an unannounced visitor. This middle-aged man in a business suit would walk into a ward and, without a word of explanation, flawlessly perform a series of acrobatic feats—handsprings, flips, and cartwheels. At the conclusion of his act he would lift his trouser legs, revealing two full-length artificial limbs. The impact was tremendous. Many who were unwilling even to try to adjust to their handicaps or to artificial limbs suddenly had a powerful motivation. In this man they saw what they could do and be despite their loss.

## B. Jesus Reveals God's Love

Because Jesus is God, the Father's divine and eternal Son, He enables us to know God for who He really is. Not only does He reveal ourselves and our potential; He also reveals the heart of God and His compassion for us despite our corruption. Through Jesus, what He is as well as what He did, we become aware of God's determination to help us, His willingness to go to any lengths on our behalf, to pay any price. By His obedience and sacrifice, Jesus provides complete and continuous pardon for all our disobedience.

This love of God expressed in Jesus Christ is the key element by which God wants to motivate us. He wants to move us with the power of His love. He could easily force us to comply with His will, but He refuses to do this. Whenever we obey and honor Him, He wants it to be because we know His love, accept it, appreciate, and return it.

## C. Jesus Liberates

By obtaining pardon for us on the cross, Jesus broke the claim and hold of Satan. He sets us free from the helplessness and hopelessness which our corruption imposes. Although Satan can still tempt, deceive, and torment us, Jesus promises that if we accept His pardon and the power of His Spirit, Satan will no longer be able to tyrannize and dominate us. This is great news— it is the gospel. This emancipation proclamation tells us not only what we are freed *from* (sin and Satan) but also what we are freed *for*. By the redemptive work of Jesus we are liberated and motivated to become more like the one who has done all this for us. We are free to begin to realize our potential as saved human beings.

## II. GOD IMPLEMENTS RECOVERY
## THROUGH THE SPIRIT

What the Father wills for us and what the Son obtains, the Holy Spirit applies and makes effective in our lives. He is the outreach of the Father and the Son. He is the agent through which they relate to us and help us. As was mentioned in the previous section, Jesus overcame our spiritual and moral corruption. In this section we note how the Holy Spirit makes this victory a practical reality in our lives.

## A. The Spirit Reestablishes and Builds the Relationship with God

The initial goal of the Spirit as He reaches out to the lost human being is to relate that person to God. Through the message of the gospel He establishes communication with God and stimulates interaction. He enables the person to accept God's love and help in Christ, that is to say, He creates and sustains faith. There is no other way for faith to begin. With our own strength we cannot fear, love, and trust God. In a state of corruption our ability for faith is destroyed. Only by the Spirit's gift and work can it be generated.

## B. The Spirit Creates and Builds a New Person

Once the bond of faith is established, the Holy Spirit launches a major rehabilitation program in the person who has been reached. Alongside the old, corrupt person, the Spirit begins to bring forth and shape a new person. The Christian, then, is simultaneously two persons—the old and the new. There is one with ideas, values, and behavior patterns that are corrupt and responsive to Satan. And, there is another with ideas, values, and behavior patterns that are Christ-like and responsive to God.

The unbeliever is only one person—the old. The Christian is two persons. These are not two separate sections of the Christian's being, one good and the other evil. It is not, for example, that the soul is the location of the new person and the body the location of the old. Rather, both persons occupy and function throughout the entire being. What are the characteristics of this new person whom the Spirit is developing within every Christian?

1. *He is inclined toward the good.* The new person who is emerging and growing within the Chrisitan reacts in a new way both toward God and toward people. In relation to God the new person delights in God's will and is able to do it. He trusts God, appreciates God, and obeys God willingly and joyfully. In relation to other people the new person has a deep concern and commitment, is determined to love and to help people regardless of the cost.

2. *He resists corruption.* In addition, the new person has an aversion to those things which offend God and hurt people. He

opposes every evil impulse and influence both from within and from without. This means that the new person is in a state of constant tension and conflict with the old person and his desires. Scripture describes the Christian life, not as a steady and uninterrupted course of improvement, but rather as a struggle, a contest, a fight, in which the new person must combat the old in order to survive and to grow.

The willingness and determination to do this is an essential characteristic of the new person. The new person is alert and opposed to every temptation that comes from without, whether from corrupt individuals or from a decadent culture. The new person is not a conformist, except to that which is from God. Stubbornly and courageously he insists on defying the immoral trends of the environment.

## C. The Spirit Dwells Within

We do not struggle alone against sin and corruption. God Himself, the Holy Spirit, is personally present within, fostering moral recovery and improvement. In order to motivate us, to move us in the right direction, and to divert us from what is wrong, God not only gives us gifts and powers, but He gives us Himself. We have a living, loving divine Person with us at all times providing the moral encouragement, support, and direction that we need. The strength and insight on which we rely are His, not ours or someone else's. We can communicate with Him; He hears and responds to our prayers and our cries as we carry on the difficult and lonely struggle of the moral life. He also speaks to us through His Word, written in Scripture and lodged in our hearts, offering us guidance, reinforcing our convictions and conscience, providing consolation and hope.

## III. MOTIVATION

What God does for us through Christ and in us through the Spirit provides us with powerful and compelling reasons for acting according to God's will. As we are reached by His love, as His forgiving and transforming work is done in us, new attitudes and values are formed which enable and impel us to become better people.

## A. Desire to Praise God

This is the supreme motivation—our love answering His. Aware of His love and grateful for it, we respond in kind. His love for us stimulates our love for Him and for others. Furthermore, out of love and appreciation grows the impulse to praise—to call attention to His goodness and greatness, to make Him and others aware of our admiration for Him and our delight in what He has done.

The purpose of praise is not to repay God, but to display His magnificence and to express our acceptance and thanks. Our obedience to God is eucharistic, a giving and a living of our thanks. This means that our chief concern as we make an ethical decision and take a course of moral action is: What decision and action is most likely to please and honor God?

To praise is quite natural, almost irresistible, when we encounter someone who is exceptionally considerate and helpful. I have a friend who, at a time when I was in great personal need, without being asked, assessed my needs and attended to them in a most sensitive and generous way. I was overwhelmed at the time and still am. I never tire of telling him and others how much this meant to me.

This type of motivation, above all, can and should characterize Christian ethical and moral response. It is the highest form of motivation. Other, lower forms of motivation discussed below are also valid and may properly function in combination with this one. However, the praise of God belongs in first place. The best and most compelling reason a Christian has for doing what is right and avoiding what is wrong is that this glorifies God.

## B. Desire to Help Others

Those who have been loved and helped by God develop the desire to treat others in the way that God has treated them. God intends and encourages this. When we want to express our love and praise He directs us to other people. All human beings need something from us; some have great and desperate needs. "As you did it to one of the least of these my brethren, you did it to me," Jesus said (Matt. 25:40, RSV). One's fellow man is the primary object of and outlet for Christian response to the love of God.

I once had some automobile problems in an out of the way place where it was difficult to get service. A stranger stopped, and with the expenditure of considerable time and effort, was able to repair the car. I felt grateful and obligated and wanted to pay him, but he refused. "No," he said, "I don't need or want your money. But I tell you what: the next time you have a chance to help someone, do it, and think of me." This is precisely what God says to those who have been saved by His love. "When you have a chance to help someone, do it, and think of me."

The Christian's second great concern in making ethical decisions, growing out of the highest concern, is: What course of action is most likely to help the people concerned? Almost every ethical decision and moral action directly or indirectly affects others, for better or for worse. Moved by the love of God, Christians want to do what is best for them. The second most important reason for doing what is right and avoiding what is wrong is that other people benefit.

## C. Desire to Realize One's Potential

Here we come to the proper place of self in Christian ethical and moral motivation. The location of self is third on the priority list. First comes concern for God, and second comes concern for others. Although not at the head of the list, self does have a high and important place. As long as concern for self remains subordinate to these higher concerns, it is appropriate and even necessary. In chapter 4 we discuss Christian selfhood more extensively. At this point we focus on the self only as it is a motivating factor, a reason for doing what is right and avoiding what is wrong.

Because a Christian believes in Jesus Christ and accepts His mercy, he knows that he is forgiven and that he has the power to become a better person. Jesus has both reconciled him to God and restored his potential for improvement. The Christian wants to make the most of this, and it is right for him to feel this way. He will not be confused and held back and pushed around by sin the way he once was.

Because of what God does for him through Christ and in him through the Holy Spirit, the Christian can grow and produce. He can become a new person. He can begin to overcome his moral problems, weaknesses, hang-ups, and conflicts. He can and he will! He doesn't want to be a spiritual and moral cripple. He wants to experience and exercise in his own heart and life the victory that Christ has obtained for him. This, too, is a good and valid reason for obedience.

### D. Awareness that God's Will Is Best

Among the great blessings of reconciliation with God through faith in Jesus Christ is a positive attitude toward what God requires. Before a person's conversion, God's revealed will is almost exclusively a negative force. It exposes and condemns the sinner. However, once trust in God is evoked through the gospel, a person is able to view God's commandments in a different light. Although the commandments continue to expose and condemn sin in Christians (the law always condemns, see Rom. 7:7–24) they also become a helpful statement of what is good for us.

Through faith in the gospel we discover that God in His law is not merely trying to boss us around, or make us jump through hoops. He desires to help us. He is our Creator, so He knows what is best for us and for others better than anyone else. His commandments are like a manufacturer's instructions for the operation and maintenance of a product. It is in our best interest that we do what He commands.

This, too, is a proper form of self-interest, which must remain subordinate to concern for God and others. It can and should be expressive and supportive of these higher motives rather than in competition with them. A Christian can honor God and demonstrate His love and wisdom by faithfully and gratefully doing what He says. Furthermore, a Christian can be sure that what he does is best for others, too, if he orders his relationships by God's commandments. God knows best!

### E. Awareness of Rewards and Punishments

God promises to reward the person who obeys. In Scripture He indicates that often (though not always) happiness and success will come in this life to those who conform to His will, and He absolutely guarantees special recognition to them hereafter. It is important to note what these rewards are *not,* as well as what they are. They are not forgiveness of sins and eternal life, for such supreme blessings can never be earned by good behavior. The blessings that are given as rewards for obedience, though valuable and desirable, are of a much lower order. Furthermore, God also warns that punishments will follow disobedience. In this life misery, loss, and failure almost always strike the person who defies and violates God's will. Hereafter, retribution is certain.

Awareness of rewards and punishments should serve as motivation only in an indirect manner. By alerting us to them, God is not so much trying to move us to action as to reassure us, to overcome our hesitancy. He is, in effect, telling us that we do not have to be afraid to obey, even if it is difficult or costly. We will not lose or be hurt by our obedience, at least in the long run, because He rewards obedience and punishes disobedience. Obedience that is primarily in response to rewards and punishments is not pleasing to God and, therefore, not rewardable. He wants us to obey for His sake and for the sake of other people, not for the rewards.

## F. Fear of Disobedience and Its Consequences

To disobey God, that is, to neglect or hurt other people, to surrender to the corrupt elements in and around us, is to jeopardize our relationship with God and risk His judgment. The Christian realizes this and fears it. Disobedience and immorality can be disastrous. To violate or disregard the will of God is a gamble in which the stakes are immeasurably high. Although every act of sin does not destroy faith and result in damnation, almost any sin can have this effect. Sin is not a harmless amusement or plaything. It is a serious threat to our ultimate well-being. We should not confuse God's mercy and patience with softness. Writing to Christians, Paul says, "Do not be deceived; God is not mocked, for whatever a man sows, that he will also reap. For he who sows to his own flesh will from the flesh reap corruption..." (Gal. 6:7–8, RSV).

Fear of relapse and its consequences is, obviously, a low level of Christian motivation. It is, in fact, the lowest. However, it is a necessary factor because of our continuing sinfulness, our dangerously strong attraction toward that which is evil and forbidden. Such motivation can never move us in the right direction, for only what is done out of love, not fear, is acceptable to God.

However, this kind of fear may check our drift in the wrong direction. In a weak and rebellious Christian, fear may still be functioning even after love for God and others has become virtually inoperative.

Some years ago I was pastor of a little congregation on the Lower East Side of New York City. One of my members, a poor and not very bright woman, had not been in church for a while so I went to see her. I asked her about her absence and she said bluntly that she was tired of being good, taking care of her children, being faithful to her husband, and coming to church. These things were no fun. Fun was doing what she felt like doing, such as picking up men in bars and sleeping with them. I tried to appeal to her love for God and for her family, but there was not much response. Finally, in exasperation I said, "Dorothy, [not her real name] how would you like to go to hell?" Startled and obviously frightened she assured me that she would not like that at all. "Well," I said, "with your attitude and behavior, that is exactly where you are headed." This sharp warning and the fear of hell stopped her short. It provided the opportunity for a further ministry, resulting ultimately in her repentance and the straightening out of her life on the basis of higher motives.

Motivation is an essential factor in ethical decision and moral action. God is at least as interested in why we do something as He is in what we do. Proper ethical instruction and healthy moral development involve concentration on the higher levels of motivation. Although lower motivations are also valid and may be used when the situation requires them, the goal is to move from the lower to the higher levels, to emphasize the best reasons that we have for doing the will of God.

*model, pattern,*
*rules, principles*

# 3 NORMS

Where does a Christian get direction, instruction, guidance for determining what is right and wrong? In chapter 2 we considered motivation—the compelling, moving reasons for doing God's will. But, no matter how powerfully motivated we are, we will not get very far in the right direction unless we know which direction that is. We need norms that reveal the specific content of the Christian life.

The term *norm* comes from the Latin *norma,* which means a carpenter's square or rule. This instrument is a perfectly square corner, and it enables the carpenter or builder to duplicate such a corner. It both exhibits and guides "squareness." Furthermore, it also reveals deviation from squareness. If you place the instrument on a piece of wood which has been sawed, you can tell whether or not the cut is square.

In an ethical discussion norms are those instruments which indicate and measure *moral* correctness. Frequently ethicists classify norms into several types. The most specific are *rules,* which are very practical and concrete. "Do not get drunk" is an example of a moral rule. Behind moral rules are *principles,* the more general and comprehensive directives or values of which rules are specific applications. "Eat and drink to the glory of God" is one way to express the principle behind the rule against drunkenness. Finally, there is a *basic doctrine* or theological affirmation from which the principle is derived, such as, "The ultimate purpose of life is to glorify God."

These distinctions are useful and will be employed in this study from time to time. However, the more primitive and practical concept of the norm as a model or pattern seems to communicate better what Scripture says on the subject. As will be evident, this is the primary meaning we will give to the word in our discussion.

## I. THE NATURE AND FUNCTION OF CHRISTIAN ETHICAL NORMS

What are the norms by which we Christians should live? What do these norms do for us? How do they work? Where are they located?

### A. Indicating God's Will

God has not remained silent about the kind of people He wants us to be. He has expressed Himself clearly on this subject, not only by word but also by deed and example. He has given us a vision of Christian personhood. He has conveyed a *sense,* an impression, of how we are to think, feel, and act.

The directions or norms that He has given us are more like the counsel and example of a parent than, for example, like a tough set of laws given by a dictator to his subjects. These directions describe concretely the kind of persons we can and should be. They are far more than an abstract set of moral principles, rules, or virtues. These norms are not ends in themselves, but are means by which God gives us a vision of the character and values which He wants to form in us.

### B. Reflecting the Needs of Human Nature

The God who made human beings knows us better than we know ourselves. He knows that certain types of behavior are destructive and that other types are beneficial to us individually and collectively. He incorporates these insights into human nature in the biblical ethical norms. He commands and requires what is best for us.

His norms are not arbitrary and they are not punitive. To repeat the analogy used in chapter 2, they are the manufacturer's guidelines for the proper operation and maintenance of the product. There are exceptional situations in which these norms do not appear to be good and helpful, in which conforming to them might even appear to be harmful and unjust. However, in the long run and on the whole, their validity is sustained. Even if, in an extreme case, an exception must be made, the exception does not negate the rule.

## C. Revealed by the Holy Spirit

Even corrupt and fallen human beings possess an intuitive sense of what God requires, a lingering realization of right and wrong. However, this perception is fragmentary, incomplete, obscured and darkened by sin. To compensate for this, God has clearly and powerfully revealed in the Bible what human beings should and should not do. He specifically defines good and evil, commands good behavior, and condemns what is evil.

Although written by men, the Bible is the authentic and authoritative Word of God. Its primary purpose is to communicate the Good News of forgiveness through the blood and death of Jesus. However, an important subordinate purpose is to reveal ethical norms, to give us an understanding of God's will for our lives.

## D. Complemented by the Spirit's Guidance

God is the source of ethical norms. He, not we, decides what is right and what is wrong to do. Through the Holy Spirit He has given us the Bible, in which there are down-to-earth, specific ethical guidelines. However, the Spirit gives us more than a book to rely on—even more than an inspired and inerrant book. He also gives us Himself.

The Holy Spirit is personally present and active in the inner being of each Christian. One of the important functions that He performs is to help the Christian know and understand the

Father's will. We do not have only the letter of the law, we also have the living and personal direction of the Spirit from within. God's written will and the personal guidance of the Spirit are not at odds with each other. They function in a complementary manner. The ethical norms written in the Scripture are the work of the Holy Spirit through the biblical authors. Furthermore, the inner guidance which the Spirit gives is consistent with and explicative of these written norms.

## E.  Counteracting Corrupting Influences

As we try to follow our natural knowledge of God's will and even the inner guidance of the Spirit, we are constantly being confused and misdirected by the forces of evil in and around us. They lead us to rationalize, to convince ourselves at times that evil is good and that good is evil. They lead us to ignore or evade the Spirit's guidance. This accounts for much of the ethical confusion we experience and much of the immoral conduct into which we lapse.

Through the written norms of Scripture the Holy Spirit clears away much of this confusion and exposes the rationalizations to which we are inclined. For example, for the Christian who is toying with the idea of having an illicit sexual relationship on the grounds that it would really be a loving and beautiful thing to do, that no one would be hurt by it, that both parties would only be enriched and helped, that the act would actually be a grateful celebration of God-given sexuality, all such attractive and plausible fabrications are shattered by a clear, strong biblical norm: "Thou shalt not commit adultery."

## F.  Fixed Points of Reference

To find your way across a body of water or a wilderness area you need some fixed points of reference—a star, a distinctive mountain peak, an island, or a reliable compass. Christian ethical norms function in the same way. They are not road maps which chart each foot of the way, or complete blueprints of the Christian life. Rather, they are reliable signposts and markers in strategic areas of life indicating the direction in which we are to go.

The Christian life is a journey through strange, confusing,

and often dangerous terrain. The world in which we live changes rapidly and drastically. We are faced with many new and difficult moral decisions. We are confronted with a wide variety of ethical opinions and moral practices, many of which are contradictory. It is all too easy to become disoriented and to lose our way. In the midst of all this change, confusion, and contradiction, God has established some definite and permanent guideposts. If we fix our attention on them and follow them, we will not wander far afield, but rather will be moving in the direction that God wants us to go.

## II. BIBLICAL FORMS OF ETHICAL NORMS

Where in the Bible do we find these divinely revealed ethical norms? How are they expressed? In what forms do they appear? What is their essential context?

### A. The Ten Commandments

The Bible contains a great deal of ethical instruction and many moral directives. From Genesis to Revelation we find material which may be classified as ethical norms. A convenient and authoritative summary of this material is given is the Ten Commandments (Exod. 20). Both Jesus and Paul employ the Decalogue in this way, as a summary. Jesus' Sermon on the Mount (Matt. 5—7) is, in some respects, an interpretation and intensification of the Ten Commandments. The same can be said of many sections in the New Testament Epistles which are devoted to moral guidance.

Ethical instruction is not the main purpose of the Ten Commandments. God's law is, first of all, a diagnostic instrument to expose and condemn sin in preparation for the gospel. However, to the person who is forgiven and empowered by the Holy Spirit through faith in the gospel, the law is also a moral guide, a norm for Christian behavior.

### B. Love As Biblical Norm

God expresses His will for our lives in many ways. These requirements are pulled together and stated briefly in the Ten

Commandments. But it is possible and appropriate to express His will for us even more concisely than the Decalogue does. Both Jesus and Paul make it clear that *love* is the essence of the commandments of God (Mark 12:30–31 and Rom. 13:9).

The Ten Commandments and all other biblical ethical norms are, in the final analysis, simply describing different ways of acting in love. They are specific and concrete explanations of what it means to be loving in a variety of relationships and circumstances. As was mentioned in chapter 1, God made us in His image, to be like Him. Since His character and conduct are manifestations of love, ours are to be also. In a word, His will for us is that we love. Love manifests itself in many different forms; in the various biblical norms God describes and prescribes what love will do.

## C. Christian Imperatives

The moral instructions of the New Testament addressed to believers may be termed "Christian imperatives." The form of these imperatives as well as their contents are very similar to the Decalogue. Like the Old Testament commandments, these New Testament imperatives express God's will for the lives of human beings, and they express this will in terms of, "Do this!" and "Do not do that!" However, there are some significant differences between the Decalogue and Christian imperatives.

Christian imperatives are combined with or based upon gospel affirmations. At times, though to a lesser degree, the Old Testament also attaches gospel motivation to statements of God's will. In the case of the New Testament imperatives, however, the relationship to the gospel is much more explicit and emphatic.

This is an important point, and a rather difficult one to explain and to grasp. To say that gospel motivation is combined with a statement of God's moral will is not meant to suggest a confusion of law and gospel. In a Christian imperative the law (imperative) and the gospel remain distinct. Although they function together, gospel does not become law, nor the law gospel. The imperative element remains a statement of God's unbending will. As such, it continues to reveal and condemn our sins.

The law *always* condemns. To an unforgiven sinner the law *only* accuses, but to the sinner who is forgiven and transformed by faith in Jesus Christ, the law of God *also* informs and instructs in good works. To those who believe and are motivated by the gospel, God's expressed will becomes a helpful guide for moral living and a statement of their potential as new persons in Jesus Christ. "Thou shalt" becomes also "Thou mayest"!

What in this presentation is called "Christian imperatives" is really nothing other than God's law proclaimed to Christians for moral instruction, along with the gospel motivation which enables them to begin to be and to do what God requires. As was explained in chapter 2, only the gospel of God's love can implement the kinds of changes which God wants to bring about in us. The law has no power to change us in a way that makes us acceptable to God. In Christian imperatives God's commands are expressed along with the motivating message of His love. An example of a Christian imperative taken from the New Testament is, "Be kind to one another, tenderhearted, forgiving one another [imperative], as God in Christ forgave you [gospel motivation]" (Eph. 4:32, RSV).

It is essential in this connection to keep in mind what justification and sanctfication are and how they are related. Justification is God's gift of pardon for the sake of Jesus Christ. Sanctification is God's gift of new personhood, also for the sake of Christ. Both are vital elements of the gospel. They are always given simultaneously. You cannot have one without the other. It is as much a part of the Good News to say, "Through God's grace you can change for the better," as it is to say, "Because of what Jesus did and endured, God does not hold your sins against you."

This does not mean that justification and sanctification are equally important. In the Christian message, justification is preeminent. God changes people for the better because He forgives them, but not *vice versa*. Sanctification is a result, not a cause, of justification. However, this does not mean that sanctification is optional or dispensable. It is an integral part of the gospel. To present New Testament imperatives as new possibilities which are part of God's gracious work in the believer is simply to proclaim God's gift of sanctification.

## D. Examples from Scripture

Not only expository and hortatory sections of Scripture, but also historical and biographical sections contain guidance for the Christian life. Ethical norms, both positive and negative, are embodied in these biblical descriptions of persons. Lydia, for example, is a model of generosity (Acts 16:15), Abraham, a model of faith (Rom. 4), and Peter and John models of boldness in witnessing (Acts 4).

Material of this kind, however, must be interpreted very carefully, for the Bible is realistic in its portrayals. Even the heroes of faith are presented along with their faults (Abraham, Moses, Samson, Peter, James, John, and so on). And the villains are sometimes described as having some commendable traits (Egyptian neighbors of the Israelites at the time of the Exodus, Pharisees, Herod Antipas, and so on).

What God approves and disapproves in these people is not always made explicit. Moral examples in Scripture are, generally speaking, more illustrative than definitive. They must be understood, verified, and interpreted in the light of the Ten Commandments and Christian imperatives. To attempt to derive an ethical norm only from an example, without clarification and support from an explicit biblical command, is questionable.

### E. Christian Traits

In many places the New Testament writers describe and commend certain attitudes, values, and virtues which are characteristically Christian. We are presented with certain traits and told that this is the way Christians are and should be. Explicitly or implicitly it is indicated that these traits are both gifts of God's grace and goals toward which we are to strive. We are to try to be this way and can to some extent become this way because of God's justifying and sanctifying work.

For example, Paul speaks of the "fruits of the Spirit": love, joy, peace, patience, kindness, goodness, faithfulness, gentleness, self-control (Gal. 5:22), and "the mind of Christ," which is characterized by self-emptying humility, sacrificial service, obedience unto death (Phil. 2:1–11). In both passages Paul not only describes what is already in the Christian, but also what ought to be there.

In the Beatitudes, Jesus also pictures and promotes distinctive Christian attitudes, values, and behavior. Those are blessed, He says, who are poor in spirit, mourning, meek, hungry and thirsty for righteousness, merciful, pure in heart, peacemakers, persecuted for righteousness (Matt. 5:1–10). Statements such as these (and there are many others in the New Testament as well) are not intended as complete descriptions of Christian behavior, or a total system of Christian values and virtues. Rather, they appear to be significant, powerful, provocative *sketches* of Christian personhood. They are more like portraits than photographs and more like artistic, literary statements than clinical, scientific statements.

However, they are clearly meant to serve, in some sense, as ethical norms. They provide us with a vision, a model, of the kinds of persons which we can and should become because of God's gracious work for us and in us.

## III. LIMITATIONS OF SCRIPTURE ETHICAL NORMS

The ethical norms revealed in Scripture, though valuable, reliable, and authoritative, are not exhaustive. Furthermore, they cannot always be applied directly to us and our decisions. We must be as aware of their limitations and how to respond to them as we are aware of their importance and potential. It is as much a mistake to expect too much of these norms as it is to expect too little.

### A. Scriptural Norms Do Not Cover All Situations

In the Bible God has not answered all of our ethical questions, nor has He resolved all of our moral problems. Many issues with which we struggle simply were not present in biblical times. Contraception, genetic manipulation, "easy" abortion, prolongation of the dying process, women's liberation, social responsibility in a democracy, management and labor disputes, complex economic problems, widespread environmental pollution—these are only a few of the moral issues which are unique to the modern era.

Rapidly accelerating technological and social changes present us with an almost infinite variety of new possibilities, many of which include unprecedented and bewildering moral problems. Scripture simply does not speak directly and unequivocally to all of these issues. God has, in fact, left many areas of life uncharted, and these areas appear to be increasing.

Why has God permitted this to happen? Why has He not

supplied us with a set of norms complete enough to cover all moral issues which we might ever face? Scripture nowhere addresses itself to this question. However, if we consider God's basic manner of relating to us, as revealed in Scripture, an answer is suggested. God is interested in far more than external conformity to His commands. He is interested in the free and willing obedience that grows out of love for Him. He is also interested that we mature spiritually and morally. He does not want to make all of our decisions for us. Rather, He wants to teach us how to make our own decisions freely and responsibly in such a way that they are, nevertheless, consistent with His will.

Like a parent preparing a child for life, God gives us many specific injunctions as well as some basic ethical principles, and these are binding. Furthermore, through the incarnation of His Son He has given us a living human example of what we are to be like. Together, these expressions of God's will form a model, a vision, of Christian personhood toward which we are to grow. A child maturing into responsible adulthood gains from the instruction and example of parents, not only a set of rules for living, but a developing feel, or sense, for what is right, even in new situations which the parents never faced or even discussed with the child. Similarly, God, through the ethical norms and the example of Christ recorded in the Bible, shapes and develops within us a sense of and feel for His will, which also helps us find our way through those uncharted areas of life, those puzzling new issues not covered in the Bible.

## B. Some Scriptural Norms Are Culturally and Historically Conditioned

It is incorrect to assume that every command of God recorded in Scripture is applicable to us today. Some were meant only for certain people and for specific situations. Some have subsequently been withdrawn or changed.

For example, the third commandment, requiring worship and rest on the seventh day, was reinterpreted and changed in the New Testament. Many other ritual and even some moral regulations of the Old Testament have been rescinded (Col. 2:16). They were originally given as signs and reminders pointing ahead to Christ. Now that He has come, they are no longer relevant or binding.

A different kind of example is the ancient requirement enforced by God that a man become a father by his brother's widow, if the brother dies childless (Gen. 38:8 and Deut. 35:5–10). There is no reason to believe that this rule applies in the New Testament era. It was never specifically withdrawn, but it was never reaffirmed, either. Consequently, it never became a functioning ethical norm for Christians.

Even certain New Testament regulations are generally disregarded in our day because of their changed significance. The apostles, for example, instructed Christian women not to decorate themselves with fancy hairstyles, expensive clothing, or jewelry, but rather concentrate on the inner beauty of a gentle and quiet spirit (I Peter 3:3) and good deeds (I Tim. 2:9–10). In first-century culture, the women who decorated themselves with fine colthing and jewelry projected an image of immodesty and extravagance. In our culture, although extreme decoration may project the same image, moderate use of these adornments indicates nothing more than stylishness and good grooming. Hence, few contemporary Christians follow the apostolic instructions strictly.

Finally, the commandment to be fruitful and multiply (Gen. 1:28) has a different significance in the late twentieth century on an overcrowded planet than it did at the dawn of creation when the world was not populated.

We must carefully study the moral imperatives of Scripture to determine if and to what extent they may be culturally and historically conditioned, and thus limited in their applicability.

## C. Not All Scriptural Norms Are Universally Binding

Some imperative biblical statements are clearly not intended to be taken literally: "If your right eye causes you to sin, pluck it out. . . .If your right hand causes you to sin, cut it off . . ." (Matt. 5:29–30, RSV). Other imperative statements apply only to certain people. For example, a certain group of ascetics in the Old Testament called *Nazarites* were forbidden to cut their hair, use alcoholic beverages, or have contact with the dead (Num. 6:1–5), but others were not bound by these restrictions. Also, Jesus commanded a certain rich young ruler to sell all he had and give it to the poor (Matt. 19:16), but He did not require this of all His followers. We must carefully study biblical ethical imperative statements to determine whether or not they are ethical norms for us.

## D.  Scriptural Norms Occasionally Appear Conflicting or Harmful

In some cases biblical norms appear to conflict with one another. For example, the fourth commandment says that you should honor your father and mother. However, Jesus says, "If any one comes to me and does not hate his own father and mother . . ., he cannot be my disciple" (Luke 14:26, RSV). And, although the law of Moses required that an adulterous person be stoned, Jesus forgave the woman caught in adultery and encouraged her accusers to suspend punishment (John 8:1–11). We are commanded to speak the truth (Eph. 4:25), and we are also commanded to be kind one to another (v. 32). But sometimes the truth hurts or even threatens to destroy other people. In cases like these, careful study and evaluation is necessary to determine which norm applies.

Since biblical ethical norms do have their limitations, we must learn how to discern which norms are relevant and binding and which are not. We must also learn how to make ethical decisions when there are no clear and binding norms. We must develop a strong and growing sense of what the will of God is. This can be accomplished through continuous and thorough Bible study. By close and constant contact with God's written law and the disclosure of His love we can acquire a feel, an instinct, for what God wills in a situation not discussed directly in Scripture.

This feel is not something that we create by our own powers of perception or invention, but rather the Holy Spirit creates it as He comes to us through the Word. This sense of the will of God is derived from the two basic elements of God's Word—both the law and the gospel. First of all, it is derived from that model or vision of Christian personhood based on the biblical expressions of God's will. Second, it is derived from the mind and heart of the new person being formed in us by the Holy Spirit through the message of God's love in Christ. By means of the law (norms) the Spirit constructs the model. By means of the gospel He re-forms us into the kind of people who can understand and conform to the model, even in new and bewildering situations.

In short, although biblical ethical norms have their limitations, they are not invalid or inoperative.

## IV. VALIDITY OF ETHICAL NORMS
## FOR THE CHRISTIAN

Some Christians, including some evangelicals, reject the entire concept of binding ethical norms (see preface and introduction). Those who take this position argue that biblical moral directives (God's laws) were given only to expose and condemn sin, not to guide behavior. Consequently, they say, to attempt to use the law for moral instruction is to abuse it. They also claim that because the Christian has the Holy Spirit within, he does not need written norms. The Spirit guides him directly from within; he knows what is right and wrong without external instruction. In the third place, they assert that to impose or rely upon written norms is to curtail (or forfeit) the freedom of the gospel, which is also freedom from the law.

However, both Scripture and historic Protestant theology make extensive use of God's revealed will as norms for the Christian life. Both Jesus and Paul tell Christians how to live on the basis of the commandments. Furthermore, the Reformers relate most of their moral instruction to the explanation of the Decalogue. In addition, the Spirit's inner guidance in no way obviates the value or necessity of written norms. The same Spirit who guides the Christian from within is the ultimate source of the biblical ethical norms. And, although He does instruct from within, He also instructs through the written law.

Finally, when Scripture and the Reformers speak of freedom from the law, they do not mean freedom from the law as an ethical norm. Rather, they teach that Christ has set us free from the law in three ways, none of which conflicts with or excludes the concept of the law as an ethical norm: Christ frees us (1) from the curse and condemnation of the law; (2) from the necessity of justifying ourselves by means of the law; (3) from the law's coercion. This is not freedom to ignore, reject, or violate the law of God. Rather, it is freedom to begin to fulfill the law joyfully and willingly by the power which God Himself supplies.

*the shape
of the new person*

# 4 FORMS

Norms, as we discussed them in the previous chapter, refer to something *outside* ourselves—the models or patterns for behavior which God has constructed and placed before us. Norms are expressions of God's will which create a vision of the kind of person that God wants us to be and to become.

*Forms,* as we consider them in this chapter, refer to changes which take place *inside* ourselves—the characteristics, the qualities of attitude and action, which can be expected in the person who is reconciled to God and being refashioned into His image. Forms are the profile of the new person whom the Holy Spirit is nurturing and cultivating within each Christian. Forms are related to norms; in fact they conform to norms. As God transforms those whom He pardons, He follows the pattern which He has revealed in the Bible.

In this chapter we will develop in some detail the shape of the new person God is forming within each believer. We will investigate the character of this new person in relation to God, to others, and to self. This is not just an ideal or an abstraction, but a concrete reality, an actual identity—some*one* who is emerging within and striving to become dominant. We need to be acquainted with the features of the new person so that we know which impulses and tendencies within us are God's will and work and, therefore, to be welcomed. We need to be able to recognize and to support the new person who is being formed within us.

It is important to distinguish between the new person and the Christian of whom the new person is a part. As was indicated in chapter 2, alongside the new person who is attuned to God and responsive to Him there remains in every Christian the old person, the old self, who is attuned to Satan and responsive to him. From this corrupt element within come many of the evil impulses which lead us astray and which contaminate even the best that we attempt. Very often in ethical discourse when we refer to "the Christian" we really mean the new person in the Christian. For example, we say that the Christian delights in God, loves His Word, and is constant in prayer. We mean that the new person is this way, and to the extent that the new person is dominant, the Christian is this way.

It must be remembered, however, that in every Christian there is also the old self who is in revolt against God, despises His Word, and tries to avoid prayer. These two elements within the Christian are in constant tension and conflict. It is incorrect to assume that the true Christian is immune to the influence of the old person and experiences only the influence of the new person. The tyranny of Satan and the old self is broken, but their influence is still present, powerful, and dangerous.

## I. GOD-CENTERED

The most significant feature of the new person is his God-centeredness. The life of the new person is lived in awareness of God, and rests in the promises of God. Another way to put it is to say that the new person lives by faith, and this also involves living for God. The highest purpose of the God-centered life is to fulfill His expectations, to accomplish His goals. This is a life that expresses and evokes praise to God, that calls favorable attention to Him. The first three (or four, depending on the system of enumeration) commandments and related New Testament materials are descriptive of the God-centered life of the new person. The exposition in the section which follows analyzes and applies these materials.

## A. Obedience

A natural and inevitable form of God-centeredness is obedience. In our cultural context, however, the term *obedience* often has negative connotations. It means galling conformity to resented demands, or demeaning surrender to the will of another. But to the new person, obeying God is a positive experience. It is glad surrender to a will which is recognized as higher and better than one's own.

The obedience of the new person is given, not in response to God's demands and threats (His law), but rather in response to His love and promises (His gospel). It reflects grateful sonship and creatureliness. The new person, moved and overwhelmed by God's generosity, looks for ways to show his high regard for God. One obvious way to do this is to comply with His will. In most cases we need not wonder what this is. God has stated it in the Bible clearly and emphatically.

## B. Worship

Worship is joyful communication with God and with His people. The new person, whose life is centered in God, and to whom the relationship with God is of supreme importance, senses the need for such communication and actively seeks it. When there is an opportunity to hear from God and to receive His love in word and sacrament, the new person will be drawn to it with magnetic force. He will cherish the opportunity to speak to God in prayer, to open up to Him, to share burdens, needs, desires, and joys. He will also treasure the fellowship of other worshiping Christians, will welcome the opportunity to encourage them in their faith and obedience and to be encouraged by them.

A variety of things may add to the attractiveness of worship—appropriate music, art, architecture, and drama, for example. To the new person, however, the great attraction is God Himself. To encounter God and interact with Him is the supreme delight. The worshipful response of the new person is surprisingly broad in scope. It is by no means confined to the sanctuary and to personal devotions. Ultimately, all of life and work becomes an occasion for recognizing God and for reacting with faith and with praise.

## C. Witness

The person whose heart and mind are fixed on God, who values God above all else, will share God with other people. Not out of a grim sense of duty, but in a natural and enthusiastic way, he will offer others the love and hope which God provides. The impulse to witness, to communicate the good news of Christ, is planted in the new person right along with saving faith. It flourishes and bears fruit in the form of Christ-like actions and Christ-centered conversation.

The content of Christian witness is not mere information about God, but specifically the message of pardon and eternal salvation through the life, death, and resurrection of His Son, Jesus. As it comes from the new person, witness to Jesus Christ is more than simply the transmission of facts and truths. It is also a report of personal experience and a testimony of personal conviction.

The desire to witness grows directly out of regard for God. It is the urge to call attention to His greatness and His grace, to help others notice and appreciate Him. Concern for people, for their well-being and happiness, is the other impelling source of witness. The realization that people desperately need to know and trust God moves the new person to speak the gospel and act it out at every opportunity. Ultimately, the ability to witness, as well as the stimulus to do so, comes from God. The Holy Spirit provides the new person with both insights and words to effectively convey the saving message to others.

## D. Sacrifice

Faith in Christ and devotion to Him attain their highest expression in acts of sacrifice. To sacrifice is to put God above everything and everyone else, even above self. The new person is able and willing to do this because he is aware of God's sacrifice for him, and is profoundly affected by the enormity and generosity of that sacrifice. By a life of sacrificial service to God, or, if necessary, by a martyr's death, the new person responds to the atoning sacrifice of Jesus Christ. What distinguishes this from other forms of sacrifice is the fact that the new person does this joyfully, confidently, and without self-pity. He does it for God, who is the center of his life and who has saved him by sacrifice.

## II. PEOPLE-ORIENTED

The person whose life is centered in God is automatically turned also toward other people. The vertical relationship has a profound effect upon the horizontal one. God wants our highest love and our constant attention, but He does not need or want all of our love and attention. When by faith we surrender to Him and in gratitude want to do something for Him, He directs much of our interest and energy outward to our fellow human beings. We owe Him love and service, and the new person wants to give these to Him, but He accepts very little for Himself. Instead, He channels the bulk of our response toward the needs of the people around us. To live for God includes living for people, being aware of them and sensitive to their needs, reaching out to them in the way that He reaches out to us. Faith, when it is alive and authentic, becomes active in love. The love of the new person for others is a reaction to and, in fact, an extension of, God's love for him.

Several striking qualities characterize the love of the new person toward other people. It is not simply a variation or intensification of ordinary human loves. Rather, it has divine and transcendent elements. It is a gift and work of God, a replica of God's own love as well as a response to that love. To emphasize the uniqueness of the love which God generates in the new person, the New Testament in the Greek original employs a special term for it: *agape*. Other terms (*philia, eros*) refer to other kinds of human love. However, when the New Testament writers wish to specify that love which is God's primary characteristic and which He activates in the new person, they almost always use some form of *agape*. The numerous references to love in this section are to the *agape*-love of the new person.

One of love's striking qualities is its unselfishness. Love is triggered, not by the attractiveness or the usefulness of the other, but by his need. Even those who are unlovable and undeserving become its objects. Not, "What's in it for me?" but, "What's in it for *them*?" is love's major concern.

Love is also unsentimental. Although it may include emotional dimensions, it is primarily an act of the will. The *agape*-love of the new person may not always feel affection, admiration, or desire for those who need help. It may, in fact, fear them or find them repulsive. However, if they need help, love reaches out to them. It wants to help and is determined to help, even those who are unworthy and unappealing from a human perspective.

The third striking feature of love is that it is sacrificial, willing to put the interests and needs of the other ahead of one's own. The new person cares enough about the well-being of others to sacrifice his own resources, convenience, comfort, or, if necessary, even life itself. "He laid down his life for us; and we ought to lay down our lives for the brethen" (I John 3:16, RSV).

Details about the loving, people-oriented behavior of the new person are given in commandments four through ten of the Decalogue and other materials throughout the Bible which expand on them.

## A. Respect

Love manifests itself in respect for others. The basis of this respect is, first of all, the conviction that the other is God's unique creature. Even the lowliest, weakest, least interesting human being on earth is one to whom God has given life and an eternal future. This realization evokes respect. Furthermore, every human being is the object of Christ's saving love, and this adds immeasurably to his worth.

Christ died for all people. Out of respect for Him and His work of redemption, love honors all of those for whom He has given Himself. In addition, other people are regarded as those in whom God's Spirit dwells, or in whom He could and would dwell. All this means that they are beings of value and potential, important to God and therefore deserving of esteem.

Also of great importance is the fact that people need respect. Their personal comfort and confidence, as well as their ability to function effectively, depends to a significant degree upon the amount of loving respect which they receive from others. A healthy and positive self-image is essential to happiness, and the self-image is created largely by the attitudes and actions of others toward that self. Consequently, by treating others with respect, love tries to meet one of their fundamental human needs.

As the well-known folk hymn says, "love guards each man's dignity and saves each man's pride." It is eager to support the self-esteem of the other person. A vital part of this is to build and protect his reputation. People's attitudes and actions toward that individual affect his self-esteem. This moves the new person to try to counteract gossip and slander, to cultivate appreciation for and respectful treatment of that other person on the part of all who know him.

Although love owes and shows respect to all people, it exercises a special kind of respect for those in positions of leadership. Parents, teachers, government officials, and spiritual leaders deserve respect, not only because they are human beings but also because they are God's representatives and servants. He has created us in such a way that we require leadership of various kinds. As a result of our corruption by sin, this need has been aggravated and complicated. Consequently, God has commanded that we make suitable arrangements for leadership in our midst, although He has not specified in every case the form that this should take.

Leaders render vital services. Some—temporal leaders—help to maintain peace, order, and justice in a world of sinful human beings, without which control community life would be impossible. Others—spiritual leaders—facilitate spiritual and moral growth by the communication of the gospel. Because they operate with God's own authority and carry out His purposes, we are to react to them with the respect that we owe Him.

Because they are fallible and sinful themselves, leaders do not always evoke respect by their personal character or performance. Even in such cases, for God's sake, we are to show them loving respect. We are to obey them, except when they issue commands which conflict with God's revealed will. For love's sake as well as for God's sake we are to respect them at all times, even when we must disagree with them or disobey them.

## B. Compassion

No aspect of *agape*-love, no mark of the new person, is more conspicuous than compassion. To have compassion means literally *to feel with* the other person, to identify with the other so completely that you hurt when he hurts and you celebrate when he is happy. Compassion grows out of involvement in the lives of other people and leads to further involvement. It is the result of noticing other people, of drawing close to them, of perceiving what is going on in their lives and what they are going through. Love looks beneath the surface, behind the masks with which others so often try to cover their personal anguish and joys.

Much interaction with other people in modern life is brief and rushed. However, the new person, constrained by love, is willing to pause and be touched by the plight of those in distress, and to enter into the happiness of those who are tasting success or victory. Compassion makes a difference. The realization that another person notices my sorrows and joys, and shares them, makes me feel better. Christian compassion is not content, however, simply to feel with others. It also insists on acting in behalf of others—to relieve the hurt, right the wrong, speak the good word, or do whatever else will help.

## C. Chastity

The approach of the new person to sexuality is also motivated primarily by love. Concern for others, the desire to act sexually in the way that is best for others, is what leads to Christian ideals of chastity.

Some misinterpret chastity as the very opposite of love. They say that love is open to and accepting of others in sexual matters, and is willing to respond generously to the sexual needs and desires of others. Chastity, in the view of such people, is rejecting others sexually, or unnecessarily restricting the expression of this very basic and vital form of love.

Others denounce chastity as a manifestation of fear, as timid withdrawal from the risk of conception, detection, and infection. Such fears are unwarranted according to these critics because of the supposed ease with which conception can be prevented or terminated, and the effectiveness with which venereal infection can be treated medically. In fairness to such critics it must be admitted that too many Christian advocates of chastity have relied heavily on motivations of fear and self-interest, as if keeping oneself clean and staying out of trouble were the main reasons for living chastely.

The perspective of the new person on sexuality is informed by the Word of God. In Scripture, God makes it clear that human beings are created to sexually celebrate only one relationship—the relationship of marriage. Conversely, God states that sexual relations outside of marriage damage and deprive others, whether they realize it or not. Trusting God's interpretation of sexuality, respecting His revealed will, and eager to live sexually in the way that is best for others, the new person opts for chastity. Love for others as well as regard for God moves and guides him to reserve the full expression of sexual love for marriage.

Chastity is not sexlessness, or anti-sex. In fact, it represents an affirmative and appreciative view of sexuality. It recognizes sexuality as a good gift of God, with great potential for contributing to human joy and fulfillment. However, it also realizes that, like every other aspect of our humanity, sexuality is corrupted by sin, which inclines us toward its misuse. Limitations placed on sexual expressions reflect respect, not contempt, for sex.

### D. Honesty

The new person, because he is concerned about others and wants to live for them, is also honest with them, both in word and deed. Stated most simply, to love is to help, and one does not help others by depriving them of their possessions or by deceiving them. Rather, love respects and protects what belongs to others. Love is unwilling to cheat in business transactions or to profit by the mistakes of others. It renders the full measure of service for which an employer or customer pays.

In addition, by its very nature, love cherishes relationships with other people. Because relationships thrive on good communication and because communication depends on trust, love protects and strengthens lines of communication by speaking and acting truthfully. Here, too, the overriding motivation is love. Not self-interest (as in "Honesty is the best policy"; i.e., honesty is advantageous), but consideration for others is the basis of Christian integrity and truthfulness.

### E. Forgiveness

To love others, and to live for them, inevitably involves forgiveness. One is constantly being wronged by others, neglected, cheated, slandered, and abused in various ways. Instead of retaliating, love wants to help the wrongdoer. Love views the wrongdoer not as an enemy to be reviled, punished, or destroyed, but as a casualty, one who has been captured or disabled by sin and is in need of rescue. To help, one must first forgive, and extend to the offender the same kind of forgiveness that

God offers. Forgiveness drains the bitterness out of the victim and frees him to act constructively toward the one who has hurt him.

The new person can be forgiving because he is forgiven. God's complete and continuous pardon for the sake of Jesus' atoning sacrifice impels and enables him to respond similarly to those who have turned against him. This forgiveness does not wait for an apology. It forgives immediately and entirely. However, as in the case of God's forgiveness, it is not fully beneficial to the offender until he recognizes his wrong, repents of it, and accepts the offered forgiveness.

## F. Generosity

Love does not carefully measure out its kindness and help, for it would rather make too much allowance than too little. In thought, word, and deed love wants to give the other person a break, the benefit of the doubt. Confronted by human need of any kind, love is willing to extend itself, and even to overextend itself. It views time and material possessions not primarily as sources of personal enjoyment, but as resources with which to help others. Confronted by questionable behavior in other people, instead of imagining and suggesting the worst, love offers the kindest interpretation that honesty will permit. Generosity which issues from and mirrors God's own is a beautiful quality of the new person.

## G. Justice

Every human society is riddled with injustices. In ways both subtle and overt, the strong exploit and threaten the weak. The demands of the many conflict with the rights and needs of the few. Like God, the new person has a special concern for the victims of injustice. He is aware of their vulnerability, sensitive to their indignities, angry at their oppressors. Although he also loves and serves those who are advantaged, the new person feels committed especially to the cause of the disadvantaged.

Scriptural support for this is found particularly in the Minor Prophets of the Old Testament and the words and example of Jesus in the New. The biblical concept of justice is not simply to treat everyone impartially, nor is it to do the greatest good for the greatest number of people. Biblical justice, rather, redresses the grievances of those who are downtrodden. The balance is actually tipped in favor of the disadvantaged.

## III. SELF-ACCEPTING

Much popular psychology and philosophy encourage excessive preoccupation with self, leading to what has been called "the new narcissism." Some evangelical theology and piety, on the other hand, have promoted a posture toward self which is excessively negative, even destructive.

There is a proper place for self in the perspective of the new person. It is not first place, for God comes first. God is and should be loved above all else. Neither is it second place, for the fellow human being, the neighbor, is and should be next on the priority list of the new person. The proper place for self is third, as far as the new person is concerned; and that is still a very important place. The well-known acrostic expresses it correctly: *Joy*—*J*esus first, *O*thers second, and *Y*ourself third.

Two observations are in order. One is that self does indeed belong on the list. The other is that the result of establishing and following this priority is joy, not frustration or debasement.

God has given the Christian the best possible reasons for maintaining positive attitudes toward self. These reasons are summarized in the three articles of the Apostles' Creed. They are essentially the same reasons why we can and should respect other people, referred to earlier in this chapter.

Because God has made the Christian a unique individual and endowed him with an endless future; because He has rescued him from sin at so great a cost; because He dwells in him through the Holy Spirit and can work through him to do great things for Him and for others—because of all this, the Christian can and should accept himself, respect himself, forgive himself, even love himself. Until and unless he accepts himself, he is seriously handicapped in his attempts to accept and serve others. A shriveled, dejected, and love-starved self is too distracted by its own needs, and desperate to try to meet them, to be able to concentrate on others and to do much for them. There is a sense in which it is true that before a Christian can love others, he must be able to love himself.

Unfortunately, a false conclusion and strategy can be drawn from this: in order to become more loving toward others, he will first of all have to work much harder at loving himself. He will do more for self, say nice things to himself and about himself. He will cater to his interests and desires. After he has loved himself a great deal more than usual, he will automatically become more loving toward other people.

Although superficially plausible, this approach operates with a fundamental fallacy, the fallacy that we can produce self-love in ourselves. The truth is that sound and healthy self-esteem is a gift from others, based on their attitudes and actions. Only the person who has been loved can love self and others. We cannot build our own self-image, except in a limited way. Others must do this for us. In this matter the Christian has some tremendous advantages. In addition to the love and acceptance which most can count on from family and friends, the Christian has the support and fellowship of the Christian community. And above all, he has the love and acceptance of God.

This is the ultimate basis of the Christian's self-acceptance and self-image. The attitudes and actions of other human beings toward us are important and do affect us. However, their value and validity are limited. Sometimes others react to us in cruel and inappropriate ways. They may deprive us of the support that we need and even punish us for doing what is right. God, on the other hand, is completely reliable and loving. Although others may ignore or despise us, He always notices and cares. When He judges and disciplines us, it is always because we need it, and because He wants to pardon and reform us. For the nourishment and development of self-esteem, the new person turns above all to the love of God and His great work.

Christian self-esteem is a large subject with many facets and dimensions, only a few of which have been selected for discussion here. Furthermore, it should be noticed that self-acceptance and self-care are not ends in themselves. Rather, they are valid and important because they are done primarily for the sake of God and for others, and not just for self.

## A. Appreciation

A Christian can and should appreciate himself. He can honestly and comfortably admit that he has assets, abilities, and achievements. Arrogance is wrong, however, for whatever he has acquired or accomplished is God's good gift and work in him. Not the Christian, but God deserves the credit. However, he need not disparage or despise himself, nor pretend that he is a zero. That, in fact, would be ungrateful, a failure to acknowledge what God has given him and done for him. Perhaps more clearly than any other biblical writer, the apostle Paul expresses this appreciation of self in the light of God's grace:

> But by the grace of God I am what I am, and his grace toward me was not in vain. On the contrary, I worked harder than any of them, though it was not I, but the grace of God which is with me (I Cor. 15:10, RSV).

## B. Confidence

Because of God's generous gifts and sure promises, the Christian can expect to accomplish significant things for Him and for other people. No matter how ominous or discouraging a situation may be, the Christian has grounds for boundless optimism. He cannot surrender to a sense of futility, at least as far as his personal potential is concerned. "I can do all things in him [Christ] who strengthens me" (Phil. 4:13, RSV). The Christian does not have to be pessimistic, or run scared through life. He does not have to shrink back from large or risky challenges. He does not have to play it safe all the time. He does not have to be paralyzed by fear of the unknown. Rather, he can live and explore and work with confidence, which is really a form of confidence in God.

## C. Provision

Because he is God's redeemed creature, inhabited, empowered, and employed by the Holy Spirit, the Christian needs to take care of himself physically, emotionally, and spiritually. God's property, God's person, deserves proper care and maintenance. The Christian does not need to be pampered or indulged, for that would be materialism and worldliness. However, he does need food, rest, fun, and comfort in suitable amounts. Because material things are also God's good gifts, the Christian has a right, even a duty, to enjoy them and to show his thanks to God for them by so doing.

Provision for self is by no means the Christian's highest priority. As has been noted earlier in this chapter, service to God and people sometimes requires great sacrifice and always involves some elements of sacrifice. However, it is also true that God at times provides for His people very generously, enables them to prosper, and explicitly commands them to enjoy the abundance which He has supplied. Both testaments of the Bible are replete with such references. While some Chrisitans give way to extravagant self-indulgence, others, and this is just as wrong, feel guilty about using any of their resources for feasting, vacations, luxuries, and the like.

## D.  Fulfillment

As a human being, and especially as a new person in Christ, the Christian has potential. The aspiration and obligation to realize that potential is also part of his new personhood. God has given him natural abilities of various kinds and strengths. Through the Holy Spirit He also endows the Christian with spiritual gifts. The new person is to recognize and accept them joyfully. He is to develop them and utilize them very diligently.

God also places various opportunities before the Christian— occasions for growth, prosperity, and service. He is to take full advantage of them. His goal in all of this is to be, not primarily personal gratification and enrichment, but rather usefulness to God and to others. There is a very natural and appropriate experience of satisfaction in realizing one's potential, but to the new person that is not the most important thing. What matters most to the new person is being a good steward of God's gifts, glorifying Him, and carrying out His purposes with the abilities and opportunities which He provides.

## E.  Freedom

Jesus Christ has set the Christian free in some very significant ways. He is free from the guilt and punishment of sin, free from the curse and condemnation of God's law, free from the fear of death, free from the devil's tyranny, free from futility. This means that the Christian is not to be a driven person, running away from guilt and from a bad conscience. It means that he does not have to get caught up in the exhausting business of trying to justify himself to himself or to anyone else. Christ has taken care of all that. Consequently, the new person is in a position to respond freely, willingly, and joyfully when confronted with opportunities to serve God and people. He can serve not because he has to in order to be saved, but because he wants to in gratitude for the salvation which is already his.

As God brings forth and shapes the new person in Christians, as He reshapes our attitudes and behaviors toward Himself, other people, and ourselves, these are some of the forms which will result from the process. Those traits described above are not merely ideals toward which we should strive or demands with which we must comply. They are profound changes which God is bringing about within us.

# 5 REASON

God rarely, if ever, does for us what we can do for ourselves. As we go about making our moral decisions, He expects us to use a basic faculty that is already a part of us: reason or intellect, and its products which are knowledge and experience. He also expects us to take advantage of what others have accomplished by the use of reason, their knowledge and experience, the insights and findings of various fields of learning as they relate to our ethical decision. Psychology, medicine, sociology, and history may shed valuable light on the matter about which we are trying to make a moral decision.

Ethics may be defined as rational reflection about what is right and wrong to do. Christian ethics is not only a rational exercise or even primarily a rational exercise. Rather, it is revelational. As was indicated in previous chapters, we know not only norms and motives, but also the full extent of our corruption, not by reason, but by God's self-disclosures in Scripture and in Christ. The dominant and controlling factor in Christian ethics is not reason, but revelation. However, reason does have a role to play in this as well as in the other theological disciplines—a role which, though limited, is valuable and even vital.

## I. REASON GATHERS INFORMATION

### A. Facts

By a process of rational inquiry we can and should gather as much information as possible about the ethical problem under our consideration. We should read the available literature and consult experts in the field, if possible. Our purpose at this point is not to make a moral judgment, but to explore; not to search for answers, but to discover what the questions are.

If, for example, you are trying to make a decision about an unwanted pregnancy, whether this is a personal decision (should I [or my spouse] have an abortion?) or a social decision (should I support or oppose an anti-abortion amendment?), then find out what you can about abortion. What actually happens when an abortion is performed at various stages of pregnancy? Inquire into the medical, psychological, historical, sociological, and legal facts. To make a valid moral decision you must have an adequate understanding of the problem, and you acquire such understanding through the use of reason.

### B. Options

An extremely important part of this rational inquiry is the search for alternatives. To decide what we should do, we must first of all be aware of the range of possibilities. *Ethics, like politics, is the art of the possible.* It is futile to decide upon an option which is not really open to you. It is tragic to choose one course of action when, unknown to you, another far better and more desirable course is available. In the case of an unwanted pregnancy, for example, what are the alternatives to abortion? What are the various methods of performing an abortion? Some alternatives are morally preferable to others.

### C. Background

Another type of information and understanding essential to the ethical process has to do with the background of the people involved, and this usually involves self as well as others. My history as a person—family background, religious training, education, professional experience, and so on—all affect my perception, inclination, and reactions in any situation requiring moral decision. The same, of course, is true of everyone.

Furthermore, my personal interest or stake in the case will also have its effect. For example, if I through various influences in my background have come to believe that a fetus is a human being with an eternal destiny, or if I and my spouse have been waiting five years to adopt a child, I will probably perceive and judge abortion negatively. On the other hand, the person whose background has helped form the opinion that a fetus is merely a mass of tissue, or who is pregnant, unmarried, and afraid of childbirth, may have a positive view of abortion.

In any moral decision it is important to know the persons involved as persons so that one can appreciate how their uniqueness affects or is affected by the decision. This too is, at least in part, a rational process involving investigation, reflection, and evaluation.

## II. REASON IDENTIFIES KEY ISSUES

Beneath every moral question that we have to answer there are additional, deeper questions. These questions beneath the question are usually called "moral issues." For example, beneath the question, "Should I or should I not have an abortion?" are additional, highly significant questions of a more general nature: Does a fetus have a right to life? Is a fetus a human being? Does a woman have the right to control her own reproductive processes? Should an unwanted child be born?

This process of digging out the underlying moral issues is an intellectual exercise which requires some aptitude and training. Although it is possible to do this kind of rational analysis alone, it is probably best done in discussion with one or more concerned persons.

There are various ways to work through the basic issues. Those involved in the discussion may simply mention or list them and then briefly describe them. Or, the process can begin with a discussion of the alternatives. In the case of an unwanted pregnancy, for example, the alternatives may be: (1) abortion; (2) bear the child and put it up for adoption; (3) bear the child and keep it.

Then, reasons for each option may be listed and discussed. Reasons given for abortion might be the mother's physical and mental health, family finances, overpopulation, and the like. Reasons for bearing the child and putting it up for adoption might be the sanctity of life, the great demand for adoptive children, the right to life, and so on. Reasons for bearing the child and keeping it might be the sanctity of life, trust in God's promise to sustain and provide, responsibility to care for one's own, and so forth. These few descriptive sentences by no means give an adequate impression of the rational process by which moral issues may be identified. This is best learned by doing, the experience of serious moral reflection and discussion of real cases.

Once the issues have been identified they must be evaluated. Which reasons given for each alternative are most important? In these main reasons you will find the key issues. In a case of unwanted pregnancy the key issues might be the mother's rights (to mental or physical health and to self-determination) versus the fetus's rights (to life and protection and a relationship with God). This is as far as reason can go in dealing with moral issues. Having identified key issues, the conflicting values which constitute the moral problem, reason must rest. The final determination of which issues or values should have priority in the decision comes from beyond reason.

## III. REASON ANALYZES ELEMENTS

There are four basic elements in every ethical decision. While the decision is being made and after it has been made it is extremely valuable to analyze it in terms of these elements. Once again this is primarily a rational exercise.

### A. Goals

What is the goal or purpose which I hope to accomplish by this decision? In chapter 3 we considered norms, the ethical principles and model which God has given us in Scripture. These norms, for the most part, tell us God's will in rather general terms. As we make our moral decisions we have to translate these norms into very specific goals. We must express them in terms of the concrete problems of our lives and our world.

For example, the person faced with an unwanted pregnancy might find in Scripture the following norms: respect, cherish, and protect prenatal human life; be more concerned about the interests of others than of self; Christians should care for their own people. From these general directives the Christian might (and, I believe, should) select an alternative to abortion. The goal would be to bear the child and keep it, or, in an extreme case (unmarried mother, severe poverty, or health problems) give it up for adoption.

In this particular case, the translation of the biblical norms into life goal is rather simple. In another case, it might require a considerable amount of rational analysis and imagination. For example, if my concern with regard to unwanted pregnancy were social rather than personal—how to foster appreciation, respect, and protection for prenatal human life in our society with its permissive abortion policies, for example—I would have to think through very carefully what my specific goal ought to be.

In selecting and formulating a goal I must be realistic. If the goal is not feasible or attainable, there is little point in attempting it. After careful analysis, in this case, I might decide to work for the passage of an anti-abortion amendment. Or, if that seems unattainable, I might make my goal to try to persuade young people, especially women, to adopt a pro-life position.

God gives us ethical norms by revelation in Scripture, many of them general in nature. Converting these into specific life goals requires rational effort—analysis, interpretation, and application.

## B. Means

Once I have specified my ethical goal in a given situation, I have another vital decision to make. How will I accomplish that goal? What means will I use to attain it? This decision, too, is made largely on the basis of rational thought and study of the views and experiences of others. First, I inquire into the available means for accomplishing my goal. I assess their probable effectiveness. I also evaluate them morally, for it is true that the end does not justify the means. It is wrong to try to accomplish even a very good goal by a means which is evil and unworthy. My means no less than my goal must conform to the will of God. This analysis and evaluation of means is the work of my intellect, my reason.

If I (or my spouse) decide to bear and keep the child of an unwanted pregnancy, we must still decide how best to go about this. What spiritual, emotional, and financial resources can provide needed support? What arrangements in the home and family can best accommodate mother and child and promote family unity? These are practical, rational decisions.

Or, in my social concern about abortion, if I decide to work for an anti-abortion amendment, how will this be best done? By contributing money, becoming active in a pro-life organization, writing letters to legislators? Or, if I decide to try persuasion (instead of legislation), what is the most promising way for me to do this? By contributing money, giving public addresses, writing pamphlets, articles, books, working in youth groups? Rational inquiry and reflection assist me in the selection of means as well as in the definition of goals.

## C. Motives

Motivation for Christian moral behavior does not come from human reason. As we noted in chapter 2, it is the gift and work of God. In fact, the dominant motivating factor operating in the Christian is to be God Himself, the Holy Spirit. As we decide and act morally, however, other types of motivation also affect us and may even dominate us. Our motives are inevitably mixed and the elements of the mixture are not always evident to us. The real reasons why we decide and act as we do are often quite different from those we talk or think about.

To uncover and evaluate our motives is, in part, a rational process. As we reflect on and discuss the moral issues in a decision that we face, we can at the same time investigate the motives that relate to these issues. Hopefully, if I and my spouse decide against abortion and in favor of bearing and keeping the child it will be primarily out of regard for God and His will, and out of love for the fetus and others. However, other, less worthy motives may also enter and even take over—the desire to avoid feelings of guilt, the desire to evoke sympathy and admiration in others, or a martyr complex.

Or, if I decide to participate in anti-abortion or pro-life campaigns, this might, in part, be motivated by hatred of women, exhibitionism, or a messiah complex. Thoughtful introspection and the assistance of wise and perceptive counselors may help me to discover sinful and unworthy motives and the need for strengthening appropriate motives.

Reason cannot correct or strengthen basic Christian motivation. That can be done only by the Holy Spirit. However, reason can discover and understand motives, and that is a vital preliminary step.

## D. Consequences

On the basis of research and reflection one can also reach an understanding of the probable consequences of moral decision and action. While consequences are not the only criteria of the moral quality of an act, they are an important consideration. To know what I ought to do in a given case I should try to determine what is likely to happen as a result of the alternatives under consideration. By a study of similar cases as well as the case at hand I should be able to estimate the consequences as fully as possible—long range as well as short range consequences, indirect consequences as well as direct ones.

What effect, for example, does abortion have on mothers, fathers, families, the medical profession, society in general? What effects can be foreseen on all of these as a result of bearing children of unwanted pregnancies? On the basis of the unique factors of this case—the particular persons and circumstances— what consequences are most likely? To decide and act without sufficient regard for consequences would be, in most cases, totally irresponsible.

## IV. REASON FORMULATES PRINCIPLES AND RULES

### A. Reason and Revelation

Human reason is not the source of the principles by which Christians should make moral decisions. The source is God and His revelation in Scripture. Indeed, there is a certain inborn sense of right and wrong which reason can recognize and to which it can respond. However, this natural knowledge of God's law is both fragmented and distorted, and the response of human reason to it is also unsatisfactory. To know what we should do, as was explained in our discussion of norms, we must consult Scripture.

The study of Scripture is, in many respects, a rational process. It is a matter of understanding words and sentences, of interpreting and relating concepts, and of applying them to life. The study of Scripture also involves literary and historical analysis.

In this study of Scripture reason must not be put above God's revelation; we must not attempt with reason to criticize or improve upon the content of revelation. Reason must remain the servant of revelation, humbly trying to perceive, assimilate, and communicate the content of God's Word. Even when confronted with difficulties and apparent contradictions in Scripture, reason is to remain in its position of humble servitude.

Limited though it is, the role of reason in the study of Scripture, and specifically in the identification of ethical norms, is a vital one. To conclude what Christians should and should not do in the twentieth century from what Scripture says and implies about right and wrong is a challenging and sensitive intellectual task. It is, of course, far more than merely an intellectual task. Ultimately, the Spirit Himself opens the Scripture and communicates its meaning to us. However, He does this, not apart from, but through serious and thoughtful study.

As we search Scripture for moral direction, we should also take advantage of the learning and wisdom of others. We should consult pastors, professors, biblical scholars, and other knowledgeable and experienced believers, and consider their understanding of biblical ethical norms. We should test our own perception of God's will against theirs, and be open to the instruction and enrichment which God can provide through them.

## B. Observing Priorities

Ethical principles are derived from Scripture by a process of study and interpretation. Some of the complexities with which one must deal in carrying out this process have already been discussed. Another difficulty when considering biblical principles is the matter of priorities. Biblical materials about ethical norms are not equally authoritative. We must be able to recognize those which take precedence and let them be our primary guides.

1. New Testament material has precedence over Old Testament material. The Old must always be interpreted in the light of the New. One illustration is the statements in Deuteronomy 24:1–4 which appear to sanction easy divorce, but which should be subordinated to the more rigorous teaching of Jesus in Matthew 19:3–9. In general, only those commands and directives from the Old Testament which are reaffirmed and reinterpreted by Jesus or the apostles should be regarded as normative.

2. Clear imperatives have more authority than examples. Moral examples, both positive and negative, of what biblical characters did or experienced should be regarded as illustrations rather than as declarations of ethical principles. If a principle is stated clearly elsewhere in imperative form, an example may make it memorable or concrete. However, it is questionable to articulate a principle on the basis of an example alone. Examples tend to be ambiguous and limited in scope.

The story of Joseph and Potiphar's wife is an example of an unmarried male slave refusing to have sexual relations with his master's wife. What does this say about a female slave's response to her master's sexual advances, or a free unmarried man's response to the advances of a free unmarried woman, or *vice versa*? Examples from Scripture are best used as illustrations of principles stated clearly elsewhere in Scripture, and should not be regarded as authoritative in themselves.

3. Clear imperatives have more authority than directives inferred from doctrines. We may, and often must, infer principles from doctrines. In many areas requiring serious ethical decisions we simply have no clearly applicable biblical commands by which to go. Indeed, it is necessary to infer principles from doctrines; they are binding in that they are often our best understanding of God's will for us in a situation. We should, however, acknowledge the difference between these and explicitly stated principles.

For example, on the basis of several biblical doctrines I may and do infer the following principles which apply to unwanted pregnancy: respect, cherish, and protect prenatal human life. (How I arrive at this principle will be described below.) If I am convinced that this is God's will as revealed in Scripture, I must act accordingly and, also, share this conviction with others.

However, I should not claim that God has said in so many words, "Do not abort." This particular principle, because it is implicit rather than explicit, does not have quite the compelling authority as, for example, the commandment against taking God's name in vain.

4. Historically and culturally conditioned commands must be distinguished from those which are clearly intended to be binding for all times. Several examples of historically and culturally conditioned commands have already been given—a man should become a father by his brother's widow; women should not wear jewelry or fine clothing. This distinction requires some competence in biblical and historical scholarship—and even experts do not always agree. However, the Christian, with the best help available, must decide which biblical commands still apply and which do not.

5. Ethical principles should be based on at least several clear passages of Scripture. A deficiency either of breadth or clarity renders the biblical base of an ethical principle suspect. An isolated reference or a number of obscure references to some aspect of God's will should not be regarded as normative.

## C. Responding to the Context

From Scripture, by a process of study and interpretation, and also guided by the Holy Spirit, we seek a sense of God's will for every aspect of life. We seek ethical norms, direction, a model. We seek to discover by a process which is largely rational that which is given in revelation, in Scripture. And we can be confident that what we seek we will find, although, perhaps, with varying degrees of certainty. However, before we can articulate this sense of God's will either as general principles or more specific rules of conduct we must relate the principle to its context, the situation of the moral decision. Moral principles and rules, to be meaningful, must be stated in terms of the context, that is, in terms of the persons, problems, and possibilities which are under consideration. The context does not provide us with the substance or content of our moral principles and rules, but it will, in part, determine the form in which they are expressed. The substance comes from revelation, Scripture. The form, at least in some cases, is determined by a rational examination and assessment of the context.

Moral principles and rules are similar to, but also different from the moral ends or goals described above. They are similar in the sense that principles and rules, like goals, are expressed in terms of the life context. Like goals, principles and rules also represent movement from the general to the specific, from broad biblical norms to more particular application. The difference is that a moral goal is the purpose or objective which you select *in one given situation*. Principles and rules, on the other hand, express a perception of God's will for *a variety of similar situations*.

> *Principle:* Respect, cherish, and protect prenatal human life
> *Rule:* Do not submit to or perform an abortion
> *Goal:* I will bear and rear *this* child

We do not require moral principles and rules for all decisions. In chapter 3 we noted that the concept of *norm* may be defined as a model or pattern. From Scripture we receive an impression of the kind of persons that we as Christians are to be. The model of Christian personhood is God Himself, as revealed in the man Jesus Christ. What Jesus is and did becomes a pattern for us.

Additional details of the model for the Christian are sketched in the various moral concepts and directives presented in the Bible. This model—drawn in Scripture and etched on our consciousness by the Holy Spirit—is sufficient guidance for most of the moral decisions that we must make. Without much analysis and reflection we sense from this model what we are to do and not do in our daily lives.

However, there are some decisions so complicated, ambiguous, and far removed from matters referred to in the Bible that we can deal adequately with them only on the basis of carefully worked out principles and rules. These normative components, although derived by inference from scriptural truths and teachings, must be formulated in terms of the context.

The abortion issue may serve as an example. As was already indicated, there is, in my judgment, no unequivocal prohibition of abortion in Scripture. Easy and safe abortion was not available in the biblical era. There is no reference to the practice of abortion in Scripture. How, then, may we discover and articulate the will of God for us in this matter? I believe there is sufficient relevant material in Scripture from which we can formulate a moral principle as well as some rules about abortion. While the discussion that follows is extremely brief it may serve to illustrate a process by which ethical principles may be derived from Scripture.

That human life is the creation of God is the unanimous testimony of Scripture. Prenatal human life is specifically attributed to God's deliberate creative activity in Psalm 139:13–18. The personal interest of God and His involvement in the life and the future of the fetus are described here in moving terms. Furthermore, in Luke 1:15 the angel Gabriel tells Zechariah that the son who will be born to his aged wife will be filled with the Holy Spirit (a uniquely human experience) "from his mother's womb."

This phrase sometimes means simply "from birth." However, later in this first chapter of Luke (vv. 41 and 44), the fetus that was the fulfillment of this promise is said by his mother to have "leaped for joy" at the presence of Mary who by now was pregnant with Jesus. Since we are told that as Elizabeth said this she was "filled with the Holy Spirit," we should not dismiss her statement as pious speculation. In Jeremiah 1:4–5 the Lord assured the prophet that He *knew* him (a word signifying a close personal relationship) before he was born or even (fully) formed in the womb.

Passages like these seem to argue for the "humanness" of the fetus. God's interest in and involvement with the fetus is comparable to His interest in and involvement with postnatal life. The fetus is created, known, loved by God, capable of a relationship with Him and response to Him—factors which suggest human status. If God reacts to a fetus as to a human being, should not we do the same?

Human worth and dignity seem to be attributed to the fetus by these passages, and consequently, the fetus comes under the protection of the commandments against hurting or killing innocent human life. On the basis of such information and interpretation I arrive at the principle mentioned above: respect, cherish, and protect prenatal human life.

However, there is also a passage which appears to distinguish sharply between the value of a fetus and the value of an adult human being (Exod. 21:22). Here a case is given of a pregnant woman who miscarries as a result of an injury accidentally inflicted upon her by another person. For the loss of the fetus only a fine was to be paid to her husband. However, for injuries sustained by the mother herself, retribution was to be exacted according to the *lex talionis,* "eye for eye, tooth for tooth" (Exod. 21:24).

Although the differences in punishment does suggest that the value of a fetus's life is less than that of the mother, this does not prove that the fetus is less than human. The punishment for killing one's slave was also less than that for killing a free person (Exod. 21:20-21). However, nowhere does Scripture state, imply, or allow that a slave is less than human. Consequently, Exodus 21:22 does not undermine the principle about respecting, cherishing, and protecting prenatal human life.

From this principle rules may be formulated. Rules are specific applications of principles to concrete situations. Reflection on the principles stated above and on present abortion policies and practices yields a number of moral rules, some negative and some positive. Some examples of each are as follows:

*Prohibitions*

Do not perform an abortion (except, perhaps, to save the life of the mother).

Do not submit to an abortion (except, perhaps, to save your life).

Do not approve an abortion.

Do not support agencies that provide abortion services.

Do not neglect or endanger prenatal human life.

*Imperatives*

Regard even unwanted pregnancy as God's work and gift.

Regard even a deformed or defective fetus as God's beloved human creation.

Bear and love even the child whose conception was not desired.

Support—spiritually, emotionally, and materially—women who are coping with unwanted pregnancies.

As we have seen, the role of reason in moral decision-making, though limited, is vital. By means of rational effort we gather information, identify key moral issues, analyze basic elements of the decision, and formulate moral principles and rules. In all of this, reason must remain the servant of revelation, Scripture. We do not, but God does, through His word and Spirit, define right and wrong. He motivates us to follow His will. However, to understand, interpret, and apply this revelation to our contemporary scene is a complex and demanding intellectual task. In moral decision-making it is as wrong to use our reason too little as it is to use it too much.

# 6 RESOURCES

A key factor in the ethical and moral performance of the Christian is proper utilization of resources. The situation is comparable, for example, to educational performance. In order to do well in college, a student needs not only a good mind and self-discipline, but also good advice in selecting a college and a course of study, guidance in obtaining financial aid, competent instructors, access to library materials, the stimulus and example of other good students, encouragement from home, and perhaps help from the study skills center. By employing such resources a student of only moderate ability may do well. On the other hand, a more gifted student who is not aware of these resources or neglects to take advantage of them may do poorly. Similarly, the Christian who hopes to improve ethically and morally needs to be aware of the available resources and to make the most of them.

## I. DIVINE HELP

Once reason has done the preliminary analytical and interpretive work described in the previous chapter, we need two basic types of assistance. First, we need *direction*—help in knowing specifically what we ought to do; clarification and definition of principles, rules, and our goals. In the second place, we need *power*—the desire and strength to do what we have come to believe is right. Both kinds of help come from God. He is our resource. Whatever aids us significantly in this endeavor is either God Himself or one of His gifts.

## A. Holy Spirit

The Holy Spirit is God as He reaches out to us with help. He is that person of the Holy Trinity who links us to the entire Godhead. All that the Father and the Son do for us, and all their contacts and blessings, are through the Holy Spirit. As we make hard decisions about right and wrong and then struggle to live by them, we can draw on the personal presence and power of the Holy Spirit.

The Holy Spirit lives within each Christian, nurturing thoughts, insights, feelings, and values which conform to the will of God. He also builds and reinforces the determination that enables us to live by our convictions. Jesus refers to Him as the Counselor, who will lead His followers into all truth. This includes not only the full revelation of Christ and His redemptive work, but also perception of His will and obedience to it (John 14 and 16).

No help which the Spirit gives is more important than love, God's own love which He pours into our hearts. By the experience of His love we can learn the kind of love that we should be expressing in our lives. By loving us, the Holy Spirit enables and motivates us to love, which finally is the summary of all that God expects of us.

## B. New Person

That the Holy Spirit gives me Himself is, of course, most important. He is my principal resource. However, it is also true that He does something significant to me: He gives me a new self. Not only does He put Himself at my disposal so that I have Someone else to depend on, but he also changes me and equips me so that, in a certain sense, I can depend on myself. Because He is creating and strengthening a new person within me, I can be sure that something *in* me, something *of* me, also knows and desires the good.

Direction and motivation for the Christian life are built right into the character of the new person. To the extent that I am still in the grip of the old person, I have to be suspicious of my moral ideas and inclinations. To the extent that I am under the sway of the new person, I can trust my moral insights and impulses. The new person is a vital moral resource on which I can and should rely. Though it is located in the self, this resource has its origin and power in God, for it is the work and gift of the Holy Spirit.

## C. Fellow Christians

God also helps us through each other, through our fellow Christians. The Spirit works in and through each Christian for the other Christians with whom he is in contact. He equips individual Christians with special interests and aptitudes which enable them to be of maximum usefulness to one another spiritually, physically, and morally. For guidance and encouragement in ethical decisions and moral action, we can draw on one another. Ethical reflection is usually done most effectively in consultation with the Christian community of which we are a part. Moral strength is reinforced by interaction with conscientious and obedient believers. Wisdom, good example, support, as well as admonition when we stumble and fall are offered to us by God through our association with fellow Christians. Just as evil peer pressures erode and debilitate our morals, wholesome Christian influences strengthen and stimulate our morals.

## II. MEDIA OF DIVINE HELP

Evangelical ethics is, above all, an ethics of the Holy Spirit. As has been emphasized above, He is our supreme and central resource. Only He can provide the ethical direction and motivation that we require. At this point we address ourselves to the question. How and where do we contact the Holy Spirit for assistance in the ethical task?

In view of the explanation above, these questions may appear to be irrelevant. The Spirit already dwells within us Christians. He is producing a new person there. In addition, He reaches out to us through other Christians. Contact with the Spirit appears to be securely and permanently established. What else is needed?

The key to the answer is found in the nature of the bond between the Holy Spirit and the Christian: it is a *personal* relationship. It is more like the living tie that exists between friends or loved ones than a mechanical connection between an electric appliance and a power outlet. Personal relationships of all kinds, including the one between the Christian and the Spirit, need to be nurtured by communication and other kinds of interaction. I need to be kept aware of the Spirit's presence and power within. I need concrete expressions of His love, power, and will. I need continuous input from Him. I need to be re-energized and re-activated by conscious exposure to His testimony. I need to present my questions, doubts, temptations, and confusion to Him and work through them with Him. Not because He is absent or unavailable, but because He is present and accessible, I need conscious and deliberate contact with the Holy Spirit.

God has provided special media, special channels through which we can have this informative and strengthening contact. He does not ordinarily contact us directly. Nor does He leave it up to us to devise means by which we can communicate with Him. He has established ways by which He gets through to us and offers us the help that we need.

## A. Word of God

Verbal communication is the standard medium by which the spirit extends His aid to us. Through the Word of God, written in Scripture and expounded and applied in the community of believers, He gives us moral guidance and motivation. Evangelical Christians stress the fact that the Holy Spirit inspired those who wrote the Bible. What is not always sufficiently emphasized is the fact that He also inspires those who hear and read it. As we receive the message of the Bible we are confronted not only by information about God or from God but also by the living God Himself, the Holy Spirit.

The Word of God is a uniquely living word. It conveys Him to us in person. As the words and ideas pass through our eyes and ears into our minds, God the Holy Spirit goes with them into our inner being, there to do His vital work. No one else's word has this capability. Very good biographical and autobiographical works make the subject "live," seem very real. However, no words by or about another person actually produce that person's presence or convey that person into the reader's inner being. The Word of God does, and this makes it a remarkable spiritual and moral resource.

Obviously, we cannot explore everything that God does for us in and through His Word. Rather, we concentrate here on that which is related most directly to the ethical and moral enterprise. Three elements in the Word of God are particularly essential in this regard.

Through that element of His Word designated as *law,* the Holy Spirit reveals and condemns our corruption. Reference was made to this in chapter 1. Not only the unconverted person, but also the Christian, needs continuous and repeated exposure to God's law. For although the guilt of sin is forgiven in the Christian, some of its power remains to confuse, mislead, and tempt. No matter how strong we may be in faith or how serious in purpose, we continue to misunderstand and to disobey the will of God.

Through the message of the law the Holy Spirit alerts us to these evidences of our continuing sinfulness. He makes us aware of our desperate need for His help. Moral strength and improvement cannot take place until and unless we face up to our weakness and failure. Our problem in this respect is so serious that we cannot adequately recognize it on our own or with mere human resources. We need the help of the Holy Spirit in the Word, specifically, the diagnostic work of the law.

Once the law has done its work in us, once we have come to realize what is wrong with us morally and recognize the danger that this poses, we are ready for the application of the *gospel.* This is the Spirit's chief and favorite work—to assure the penitent sinner that he is forgiven because of Christ's atoning work. For our own good the Spirit must tell us about our sins, but His greatest delight is to tell us about our Savior.

The main subject of the Spirit's testimony in the Word is Jesus Christ. In fact, the Spirit is far more interested in telling us about Christ than He is even in telling us about Himself. His consuming purpose is to keep us aware and appreciative of the Father's love for us as manifest in the obedience and sacrifice of His Son. Not only at the beginning of our relationship with God, but throughout our earthly life, we need the Good News that because of Jesus' death and resurrection we are reconciled to God.

Through this message the spirit stimulates and reinforces two basic responses in the Christian. One is faith. That is to say, He enables us to accept God's offer of pardon and the other promises which go with it. This demonstration of God's love evokes love for and trust in God. The second basic response is the desire to please God by loving obedience to His expressed will. Maintenance of a close faith relationship with God and a strong desire for obedience are vital to moral health and strength. The gospel is the resource for both.

In addition to the law and the gospel there is a third element in God's Word of great moral significance—*norms*. Since these have been covered at length in previous chapters, we will confine the presentation here to a discussion of *norms as a resource* for ethical decisions and moral action.

One of the most difficult and frightening tasks that Christians face today is trying to determine God's will in the many issues not referred to directly in the Bible. To work through these issues responsibly we must be thoroughly informed and fully aware of everything in the Bible that speaks even indirectly to these issues. We must proceed from the known to the unknown.

Even to apply to modern life those commands that are explicit in the Bible requires extensive scriptural knowledge and intensive penetration into its meaning. Continuous refreshment and reassessment of biblical norms is essential to ethical and moral maturation. The Bible is not a computer which grinds out ethical norms on demand. It is the revelation of God's will in a form that requires faithful, patient, and diligent study. In this respect it is more like a gold mine than a computer. To discover the treasure and be able to use it, we have to be willing to search and toil. Although it is an invaluable source of guidance for the Christian life, it is not always an easy source to tap.

Finally, what the Spirit provides in the biblical ethical norms is not so much a moral code as a model of Christian personhood. It is a vision and a sense of how He wants us to feel and act. For this reason, too, it is extremely important that we investigate thoroughly and review repeatedly all that Scripture says about Christian attitudes and behavior. Only in this way will our perception of the model be as clear and complete as possible.

## B. Sacraments

The evangelical community is divided on the doctrines of baptism and the Lord's Supper. Some do not regard them as God's actions by which He conveys His grace, presence, and power. Rather, they regard baptism and the Lord's Supper as actions of believers, testimony of their acceptance and commitment to the Savior who was presented to them in the gospel. There are further disagreements over the manner of administration of baptism and the Lord's Supper, eligibility for participation, and the nature of Christ's presence, to mention only a few. One of the great tragedies of Christendom is that these ordinances of the Savior, designed to express and foster unity among His followers, have been the source of such dissension and division.

In what follows I express and confess a sacramental view with which some evangelicals will not be able to identify. However, I will attempt to do this in a way that highlights what all evangelicals hold dear, namely, the evangel, the gospel of Jesus Christ. If baptism and the Lord's Supper are viewed as forms of the gospel, their value as an ethical and moral resource is readily evident.

Paul describes baptism as a transforming union with the death and resurrection of Christ (Rom. 6). Although this is a one-time event, it has a dramatic and lasting effect. It is a powerful resource in the Christian's ongoing struggle against sin and toward righteousness. The reason for this is that baptism is a process by which the individual is liberated from slavery to the power of sin as well as from condemnation by its guilt.

Furthermore, baptism effects the crucifixion of the old self. The word *crucifixion* is, perhaps, significant in this connection, Crucifixion is a lingering death. The dying of the old self initiated by baptism is a long, drawn-out ordeal. The baptized believer still has an old self, squirming in rage and pain, fighting for life, even for release from the cross and return to control. As he experiences the influence and pressure of the old self, the Christian has a tremendous source of encouragement and confidence in baptism.

The new person does not have to be pushed around by his old self. The old self is defeated, crucified, dying as a result of the Christian's union with the crucified and risen Savior in baptism.

Nor does the Christian have to be intimidated or manipulated by sin and Satan, because he is baptized. The new person is liberated from them. This does not mean that he is free from their attacks or immune to their temptations. However, it does mean that he is free from their enslaving control, free to fight against them. Most important, baptism means that the Christian is free to enter the joyful service of his Lord and free to grow into His likeness through the power of His Spirit. For the Christian to remain aware of his baptism is to remember that he is free, which makes baptism a splendid moral resource.

When He instituted His Supper, Jesus referred to the bread and wine as His body and His blood offered for the forgiveness of sins (Matt. 26:26–29). Paul describes the elements of the Eucharist as *participation* in the body and blood of Christ (I Cor. 10:16). Clearly, through partaking of this meal, the Christian is put in touch with the elements of Christ's atoning sacrifice. Even those who do not hold to the doctrine of the real presence generally recognize the Lord's Supper to be a *remembrance* of Christ's sacrifice and the *proclamation* of His death (I Cor. 11:25–26). Like baptism, the Lord Supper's is a form of the gospel, a vivid presentation of Christ's self-giving, a reenactment of the drama of Calvary which offers the benefits of that event to the recipients.

The fundamental benefit of the Lord's Supper from which all others issue is the forgiveness of sins. Whenever and however the Lord's death is communicated to a person, it is with the purpose that he recognize and accept the pardon for which Christ died. Through His Supper the Lord wants to remind and reassure the Christian that He loves him despite his sin, that He has dealt with the consequences of his sin, that His relationship to him is still intact or can be restored. Along with forgiveness, then, comes a renewal of the Christian's union with his Lord, from whom he is alienated by sinfulness and moral lapses.

The moral significance of the Lord's Supper is profound. Its potential as a resource for ethical and moral progress is tremendous. In the Lord's Supper the Christian can find the fresh start that he needs when he is dogged by awareness of his moral weakness and defeats. In it the believer encounters the love of God, which is both the motivation and the model of the Christian life. Like the other expressions of God's forgiving love, the Lord's Supper reactivates and revitalizes the power of the Holy

Spirit within the believer. It is a refreshing, encouraging, strengthening interlude in the tough, ongoing battle of the Christian life.

## C. Prayer

Strictly speaking, prayer is man's address to God, man's response to His loving words and actions. And yet it is also a work of the Holy Spirit. He both prompts the Christian to pray and helps him to pray (Rom. 8:26–27). Through prayer the Spirit sensitizes us to His presence and opens us to His influence. The purposes of prayer are numerous and its benefits are diverse. We will focus only on those aspects of prayer which relate most directly to the Christian as he functions ethically and morally.

To a large extent, Christian ethics is an attempt to understand what the will of God is in difficult and confusing issues which are not discussed clearly and completely in Scripture. Perceiving God's will in such cases and then carrying it out in sensitive and practical ways requires an abundance of wisdom. But this wisdom is ours for the asking (James 1:5, 3:13–17). As we analyze ambiguous moral issues and deal with cases in which divinely revealed norms and values appear to conflict, we actually have the opportunity to consult with God about them in prayer.

Rational analysis and study of God's Word can and should be combined with prayerful reflection and review of the matter at hand. Item by item, in personal conversation with God, we can go over every aspect of the case. In prayer we expose our analysis, interpretation, motives, and judgments to His scrutiny and seek His reaction. In prayer we reach out confidently for the Holy Spirit's aid in formulating the decision. Our rational analysis and interpretation of Scripture must be confirmed or redirected by the wisdom which only the Holy Spirit can provide.

Sometimes even more difficult than knowing what is right is doing what is right. Here, too, prayer is a powerful resource. When great courage, generosity, or patience are required in order to live by our ethical convictions, we can cry out for them to God in prayer. He will hear and help. God often waits until we have prayed before giving us the aid that we need. He does this, not because He is unwilling, but because He wants us to recognize unmistakably the fact that this help comes from Him. Not only the clear teaching of Scripture but the experience of Christians throughout the ages substantiates this. Some of the most inspiring chapters of Christian history, current as well as ancient, are those which describe the steadfastness of Christian martyrs. Supported by the Holy Spirit in answer to prayer, they have endured deprivation, torture, and death rather than deny their Lord. Few, before facing these frightening choices and ordeals, displayed heroic qualities. However, in their extremity they prayed for moral strength, and they received it in a measure which exceeded their highest expectations. For moral strength in all situations we have the great resource of prayer.

There is indeed no shortage of resources for our moral guidance and strength. In the free world, at least, we are faced with a superabundance of them. (Even in most anti-Christian societies they are available, although at a risk and a price which are often considerable.) The Bible is published in hundreds of different languages and translations—it is more widely circulated than any other book. Christian literature and music flood the market, and Christian programs are broadcast extensively. Christian congregations and fellowships eagerly invite participation and membership. Baptism and the Lord's Supper can be obtained virtually everywhere. Prayer, a direct line to God, is open at all times to anyone who calls in Jesus' name. We have all the help that we need or can possibly use. We are, in fact, faced with an embarrassment of riches.

Furthermore, we can be confident of the complete adequacy of these resources. If we take advantage of them, we can experience significant ethical and moral success. They are powerful resources that can make a profound difference in our hearts and lives. Although perfection is not attainable in this life, great improvement is.

By drawing on these resources many Christians have demonstrated rapid and radical transformation for the better. For others progress may appear less dramatic and slower. But though the pace and form of the change may vary, the adequacy of the resources is constant. By utilizing them we can very definitely develop a clearer and stronger sense of what God wants us to do and what we are to avoid. We can stand vigorously against corrupt influences in and around us. We can move ahead in Christian obedience with confidence and consistency. God's help offered through these resources makes such obedience possible.

From this we are led to a rather sobering conclusion. Our ethical and moral failures are largely the result of our not employing the marvelous resources which God has put at our disposal. We cannot truthfully plead helplessness. We are without excuse.

A very crucial ethical decision which every Christian makes, knowingly or unknowingly, is whether or not he will use the resources which God provides to be morally strong. The alternative is to neglect them and become morally weak, or even die. God offers His help. He invites, urges, and enables us to accept, but He does not force Himself on us. We are always free to say no to Him.

Other factors also account for our moral failures, but many can be traced back to this single simple cause: we do not make sufficient use of the help that God gives.

*how to cope*
*with ethical*
*and moral defeat*

# 7 FAILURE

Failure is a recurring experience in the life of every Christian. We have referred to this briefly in several earlier chapters. The effect of repeated failure can be detrimental. Reviewing a history of his ethical and moral defeats can be demoralizing to an individual, can destroy confidence and even the desire to try. Or, it can lead to rationalization. Rather than admit failure, a person may try to explain it away both to himself and to others, and fabricate a counterfeit appearance of righteousness in its place. Both of these reactions to failure are dangerously wrong. It is essential for moral survival and growth to understand failure and to deal with it appropriately.

## I. THE CHRISTIAN AS FAILURE

Every Christian fails adequately to know and do the will of God. This is not only the problem of the unbeliever and the enemy of God, but also that of the most devout and mature child of God. Paul, for example, long after his conversion confesses and agonizes over his continued moral failure (Rom. 7:7–25).

No matter how much we care or how hard we try, we all fail miserably and frequently.

## A. Christian Disobedience

Because of ignorance or weakness we often make bad ethical decisions and take bad courses of action. Our analysis of the issues may be faulty. Our interpretation of Scripture may be inaccurate. We may misread the Spirit's guidance from within. For any or all of these reasons we often choose a course of action that is evil. The tragedy in such cases is that our intentions may be excellent. As we carry out the mistaken and evil course of action, we may be fully convinced that it is good, right, and necessary.

In other cases, even though we realize that a type of behavior is evil, we decide to do it anyway, because it appears pleasurable or rewarding. The reverse also happens. Even though we realize that a certain course of action would be good and God-pleasing, we knowingly refuse to do it because it appears costly, arduous, or inconvenient. Deliberate failure and sin are particularly dangerous.

Scripture issues severe warnings against them (Heb. 10:26–31). Such sins reveal contempt for God's grace in Christ and rejection of His Spirit. They are a serious threat to saving faith and may even destroy it completely. A term often applied to this type of failure is "mortal" sin (I John 5:16–17), because it is fatal to faith.

## B. The Imperfection of Christian Obedience

That our disobedience is failure we can understand and accept easily enough. More difficult to grasp is the paradox that even our obedience is failure, and yet this is also true. Our obedience to God is never fully what it ought to be. It is always deficient, defective, tainted. Since our obedience as well as our disobedience is failure, there is a sense in which we are complete ethical and moral failures.

Our obedience to God is fragmentary and imperfect. Even when we do our best, we never do all that He expects and requires. This is very disturbing to God, for He is satisfied with nothing less than perfection. He never gets this from us, since our performance is spotty and inconsistent. At times we may appear to be conforming closely to His will, at least externally. However, this will often be followed by relaxation of effort or a complete moral breakdown in some other area of life. We like to take comfort in the fact that, although we are not perfect, we are doing rather well compared, at least, with some people. But, this is false comfort. For compared with God and what He requires, we fall pathetically short.

The other serious problem with our obedience, in addition to its imperfection, is that it is contaminated. Our obedience to God is always tainted by mixed motives. Even when we do the right thing, it is always partly for the wrong reason. The power of sin, although forgiven and counteracted, is still present and active in us, spoiling even the best that we do. Our obedience is often grudging and half-hearted. We do what God commands, not because we want to. but because we have to.

In other words, our obedience is a response to His law instead of to the gospel, and this is unacceptable. Or, instead of obeying because we want to glorify God and help people, we may obey primarily because we realize that we will benefit from this or at least avoid trouble. Not faith and love but self-interest often dominates our motives. Or, we may begin an act of obedience with a proper motive only to have it replaced by one that is improper.

For example, I may be moved to help someone in a way that requires a large amount of time and money. Initially this may grow primarily out of genuine concern for this person. However, as the project continues I may find myself motivated increasingly by the appreciation and admiration that this act elicits, rather than by love. My motive has deteriorated. Mixed and tainted motives are a problem because God is not only interested in outward behavior. He is every bit as interested in *why* we do something as He is in *what* we do. For these reasons, even obedience which is externally successful is, in fact, a failure.

## C. The Impact of Failure

Awareness of the inevitability of failure can have a devastating impact upon the Christian. Defeatism, irresponsibility, and despair are its usual products. Many Christians are overwhelmed and effectively disabled by past and anticipated moral failures.

Since we know in advance that our obedience will be a failure, why even try? Under these circumstances Christian obedience seems to be an exercise in futility. A Christian with this attitude would say that instead of trying to obey and to improve morally, maybe we should simply accept the fact of our helplessness and concentrate on being forgiven. In other words, we might as well forget about sanctification and be concerned only about our justification. Not many Christians express this feeling openly and strongly, but most recognize it as a familiar part of their personal experience. Failure discourages ethical and moral effort.

Still more insidious is the conclusion that since failure is certain and unavoidable, we might as well go at it with gusto. A Christian may say to himself, "Since I can't win morally, I might as well enjoy the pleasures of losing. If I can't please God, I might as well please myself, abandon myself to sin, and do whatever I want." Much reckless and irresponsible behavior on the part of Christians grows out of this point of view. Even many who have not acted out such feelings have been troubled by them. Failure encourages moral laxity.

The most dangerous reaction to failure is despair of one's ethical and moral ability. Despair of this kind can easily lead to spiritual despair, to the growing suspicion or conviction that saving faith is gone. A Christian may say to himself, "If I really believed in Christ as my Savior, I would not fail so miserably and so often. If I ever had genuine faith, it is obviously gone now."

A companion of this frightening thought is despair of God's mercy. The Christian may wonder how God can forgive him if he keeps on failing. "I sin over and over again. I tell God I am sorry but still keep on doing it, sometimes deliberately. If I were God, I would not forgive a person like me." Such a Christian may be certain God has given up on him and destined him for punishment. He may be convinced that there is no way he can get back on good terms with God. "He was generous and forgiving. He gave me many wonderful blessings and opportunities, but I have blown it. There is no longer any hope for me." Consistent failure can lead to deep despair.

### D. The Cause and Exposure of Failure

The corruption of sin embodied in the old person is still very much a part of the Christian. Through faith in Christ the Christian is forgiven of it, and by the power of the Holy Spirit he is able to resist it and counteract it. However, it remains as a confusing and misleading force, a debilitating and enervating factor in the Christian's life. Every failure is symptomatic of this chronic spiritual and moral disorder.

God does not permit us to overlook or forget our failures or the underlying corruption from which they emerge. Through the message of His law, He continually reminds us of them. He keeps us aware of what is wrong with our hearts and lives as well as of the appalling consequences. He holds our attitudes and performance up against the revelation of His will, so that we become painfully aware of the discrepancies. As He does this, God is like a physician who relentlessly pursues the diagnosis of a patient and frankly discloses to him the full seriousness of his condition. In the case of a lingering or chronic illness, diagnosis is necessarily a continuing process. So is God's diagnosis of our sinfulness.

## II. GOD FORGIVES FAILURE

God calls attention to our failures, not in order to discourage or demean us, but in order to prepare us for His help. Through His diagnostic work in the law He hopes to make us receptive to the remedial work of His gospel. Although God's anger at our sinfulness is very real, even greater is His love which makes Him eager to pardon.

### A. Christ Paid the Penalty

In order to make forgiveness possible, God's own Son, Jesus Christ, personally paid the penalty for our sins. Because God takes our failures very seriously and because He wants us to take them seriously, He did not just quietly and painlessly erase them from the record. Instead, He insisted that they be paid for in full, with bitter pain, blood, death, and the experience of hell. All this His anger and justice called for. However, because He loves us and because we could never survive this penalty, He mercifully paid it Himself in the person and through the work of Jesus.

Although completely obedient to the Father's will Himself and entirely innocent of any wrongdoing, Jesus Christ accepted the blame and the burden of our failures. In keeping with His Father's saving purpose, and moved by the same great compassion, He suffered and died for our sins. By His obedience and sacrifice He made forgiveness available to us. Not our own efforts to obey, nor our regrets for failing, not the painful consequences that we frequently endure in this life on account of our sins, nothing that we do or suffer, is the basis of our forgiveness. Only because of Christ's loving and vicarious self-giving can we escape condemnation, and hope for pardon.

## B. Faith Receives What Christ Provides

God never deals with us in a mechanical or impersonal way. Having provided complete forgiveness for us through the life and work of Jesus, He does not simply apply this to us automatically. He does not, for example, simply include it in the air that we breathe or the water that we drink. He does not just instruct a computer to remove all debits from our accounts. Rather, He approaches us personally in the various forms of the gospel. He tells us how and why He wants to forgive us. He offers us pardon for our failure and invites and enables us to accept this.

The forgiveness is not ours and does not count for us, however, unless and until we make it our own by faith. Only the person who *believes* is forgiven and saved. God wants to forgive us but will not do so unless we are aware of His offer and respond to it positively. There are at least three phases to the faith response. The first is that I realize *I need Christ* and His help—I am aware that I am sinful and lost without Him. The second phase is that *I want Christ*—I desire and long for Him and His help. The third is that *I accept Him*—I count on His promise, realize that I actually possess the One whom I need and want.

From the point of view of a Christian's experience, faith appears to be his own work and doing. It consists of things that he thinks, feels, wills, and does. Scripture, however, describes faith as a gift and work of God (Eph. 2:8). Through the gospel the Holy Spirit approaches him, not only with the offer of pardon but with the power to accept it. Without coercing him in any way, the Holy Spirit penetrates his mind and heart and enables him to believe.

The Christian lives constantly in this forgiveness as long as faith is there. Some incorrectly think of themselves as jumping in and out of God's forgiveness. They feel that every time they sin they are cut off from God and His pardon. According to this interpretation, only when they consciously regret a sin and specifically ask to be forgiven of it are they restored to God and His grace. If a person dies during the interim between an act of sin and an act of repentance, he is lost, according to this view.

But there is a basic misconception here. What condemns a person ultimately is not sin, but unbelief. If sin condemned, all Christians would be lost, for its corruption remains in all of us even when we are not committing conscious acts of sin. As has already been explained, sinful behavior, especially deliberate sin, is threatening to faith and may destroy it completely. However, not all sinful acts destroy faith. As long as we have faith, even very weak faith, we are completely and continually pardoned. We have the assurance that we live in God's forgiveness twenty-four hours of every day. Even before we are aware of a sin and ask for pardon, He forgives. He lovingly and patiently puts up with our failures, He continues to love us and relate to us, as long as we have faith.

Obviously, this kind of arrangement is subject to abuse. However, it may also be productive of great incentive and strength for doing the will of God despite previous failures. This is God's purpose. Whenever we become aware of God's forgiveness, we also receive new strength from the Holy Spirit. The two—God's forgiveness and the Holy Spirit—always go together. You cannot have one without the other. God assures us of His constant forgiveness and urges us to keep returning to Him for fresh awareness of this, so that the power of the Holy Spirit will be released and activated in us anew.

This explains why the Christian must continually seek God's forgiveness in a spirit of penitence. It is not that he might be condemned for any unconfessed sin. Rather, it is through the expression of God's forgiving love in the gospel that the Holy Spirit reaches into the Christian's heart and life with strength. As we enter into God's forgiving love again and again, our love for God grows and our incentive to obey Him increases. As we experience God's patience with us and His pardon for our failures, the Spirit builds our determination to do better in the future.

Furthermore, He builds our confidence that we can improve. By the repeated application of God's forgiving love, the Spirit develops in the Christian an increasing sense of responsibility to

God and His will, as well as the kind of loyalty and commitment that prevent defeatism and easy surrender to temptation. Because the Christian has been forgiven so generously and so often, he wants to please God. Because the power of the Spirit accompanies that forgiveness, he knows that he can please God.

The following example from human experience illustrates the motivating potential of forgiveness. A certain husband cheats on his wife, even though she is warm, loving, attractive, and faithful to him, and even though he loves her as well. When she discovers this, she is angry and deeply hurt. Their relationship has been grossly violated and its survival appears uncertain. However, in spite of what he did, she still loves her husband, forgives him, and wants to save their marriage. He by this time is deeply remorseful, and is overwhelmed by her loving offer to forgive and forget. He accepts gratefully, and by this experience his love for her matures and intensifies. In their life together, every new experience of her love and forgiveness increases his affection for her, appreciation for her, and desire to be a better husband to her.

## C. God Accepts the Efforts of the Forgiven Sinner

By faith we receive pardon which covers all of our failures. As a result, they no longer appear on our records. While regret for them remains, our failures no longer terrify our consciences. Most importantly, we have the assurance that our failures will not be able to condemn us at the final judgment. Everything wrong that we have ever done, all the opportunities for good that we have left undone, every corrupt motive and inclination, is obliterated by God's pardon.

Furthermore, in the place of all of our failures and corruption, the righteousness of Jesus Christ, His obedience and sacrifice, is applied to us. This makes us and our poor obedience acceptable to God. Covered by the righteousness of Christ by faith, we ourselves and our efforts to please Him are approved by God now and will be also at the judgment. For Christ's sake our good works will be recognized and rewarded at the judgment despite their inadequacies. His perfect obedience counts for us and compensates for everything that is lacking in our character and performance.

## D. Forgiveness Dispels Pride and Despair

There is a proper kind of joy and satisfaction that Christians may feel as a result of their obedience to God. To have tried to do the right thing ought to make us feel better than to have capitulated to temptation. However, the old person would like very much to convert the joy of obedience into arrogant self-righteousness. It attempts, often successfully, to get us to smugly congratulate ourselves on our fine moral performance and to look with disdain upon others who do not appear to be doing so well. The fact and experience of forgiveness dispels this kind of pride. Forgiven persons have been made painfully aware of their failures and have been led to realize that only because of Christ's obedience and sacrifice are they and their obedience acceptable. The truth is that there is nothing in or about *us* of which to be proud.

On the other hand, because we are forgiven, despair, too, is unwarranted. Forgiveness is the assurance of God's pardon. It is also the source through which the Spirit's power surges into us. Furthermore, it includes the guarantee of our ultimate moral perfection. Forgiveness not only enables us to live with our failures, it promises us that we will not always be failures. The God who now forgives will, in the life to come, make us spiritually and morally whole and completely successful at knowing and doing His will. Disappointment over our present limitations and weaknesses is balanced by the prospect of our final victory.

## E. Forgiveness Implies Contrition and Amendment

Although God's forgiveness is abundant and constant, it benefits only those who are contrite, who recognize and regret their failures. God forgives the believer immediately according to his need. However, before that forgiveness can register with him and be effective in him, the Christian has to face up to his failures, be alarmed by them and sorry for them. The solution of God's forgiveness will not mean much to the Christian unless he recognizes his problem and takes it seriously. Sin to which he clings longingly and which he intends to repeat cannot be forgiven. As long as a believer feels that way about his sin, what he is seeking from God is not forgiveness of sin but permission to continue in sin. This God will never grant.

As preparation for forgiveness, the Christian must first experience contrition. God Himself induces this through the message of His law. He keeps hammering away with the demands and threats of that law so that, instead of being blissfully unaware of his sin or friendly and comfortable with it, the Christian becomes concerned about it and sorry for it. Contrition makes him react to his sinfulness as an enemy to be fought rather than as a game to be played or a pleasure to be enjoyed. Contrition precedes forgiveness.

Amendment of life follows forgiveness. When by faith in Christ we accept God's forgiveness, we also accept the responsibility to do better in the future. (See chapter 8 for a complete discussion of this improvement.) Anticipation of improvement and commitment to improve are necessary elements in the attitude of the forgiven person.

As the Christian accepts God's pardon, it must not be merely because he wants to escape punishment but also because he seeks rehabilitation. Anything less reflects contempt for God's forgiveness and transforming purpose. God does not lift us out of the gutter of sin and clean us up so that we can crawl right back into it again. Rather, He cleans us up because He wants to lead us in a new and better direction. He makes this clear from the outset. Unless we are also willing to accept His gift and program of rehabilitation, we have not accepted His pardon, either. The two are inseparable.

Although Christians must be realistic about ethical and moral failures, we need not be overwhelmed by them. It is essential that we face up to them honestly and acknowledge their seriousness. There is no hope or help for us until we admit that we are failures. And yet if this admission is followed by acceptance of God's forgiveness, then hope and progress are possible. Instead of being a defeated and demoralized failure, the Christian, by virtue of his pardon through faith in Jesus, is hopeful and improving. He knows that God loves and accepts him, despite his failures.

# 8 IMPROVEMENT

Although failure is inevitable (chapter 7), improvement is possible, not only theoretically, but actually. In fact, improvement is more than possible. It is necessary. God does not merely offer His forgiven people changed behavior as an option or alternative. He insists upon it firmly but lovingly, because His honor, the needs of others, and our own welfare require it. In addition, He personally facilitates this improvement.

The pattern of Christian ethical and moral improvement is not a steady, upward line. Nor is it a natural, inevitable unfolding of our potential. Rather, it is the result of struggle between the new person and the old, between the Spirit and the flesh, in which the Holy Spirit asserts the victory and lordship of Christ in our lives. The course of improvement is marked by setbacks, defeats, and relapses into the old, corrupt patterns of behavior. However, it is a real movement of self and life in the direction of God's will and should be evident both to self and to others.

Some evangelicals overemphasize our continuing sinfulness, and fail to do justice to the realities of victory and success in the Christian life. While triumphalism is a distortion of the Christian posture, so is defeatism. One does not have to be a naive perfectionist to take the prospect of ethical and moral progress seriously.


## I. THE CHRISTIAN CAN IMPROVE

This is a promise of God to be accepted by faith and acted upon with confidence. The idea that the Christian can improve is not wishful thinking or an unattainable ideal. It is a live option, a viable alternative. We have said that ethics is the art of the possible. To the Christian, ethical and moral improvement is possible. Part of the mindset of the new person whom the Holy Spirit is shaping within him is a cautiously optimistic view of his potential for conforming more closely to the will of God.


### A. Free to Obey

The Christian has heard God's own emancipation proclamation in the gospel. He knows that he has been set free from the bondage to sin and Satan. He realizes that he is no longer helplessly and hopelessly trapped in corruption. As a truly liberated person he is in a position to say yes to God and no to that which goes counter to God's will.

This concept of freedom differs sharply from many current notions of freedom. In our day, liberation movements define freedom, at least partly, as the power to say no to others and to be controlled by one's own will and interests. To the Christian, however, the highest and best freedom is the opportunity to submit to the will of God, to find fulfillment in obedience to Him. This freedom is not a natural endowment. We are born in captivity to the worst elements in and around us, deprived of the joy of an obedient relationship to God, and doomed as a result. Through God's act of deliverance in Christ, we have been rescued and released. Consequently, we are able to develop more Christ-like character and conduct. We are free to begin to obey and to improve in our obedience.


### B. Justified

Another reason why the Christian knows that he can improve is that he has been justified by God. The guilt and punishment of sin which otherwise would defile and render unfit every attempt to please God have been removed. Through the blood of Jesus which was shed for him, the Christian is cleansed of all that makes him and his works offensive to God. In addition, he knows that he is clothed with the righteousness of Jesus Christ. Everything right and good about God's Son, especially His perfect life and innocent death, is applied to the Christian by faith. The justified person knows that he has what it takes to become a better person in God's sight. The greatest obstacle to moral improvement is the guilt and punishment of sin, and God has dealt effectively with both.

## C. Sanctified

The third reason why the Christian knows that he is capable of making moral progress is that he is being sanctified. This, too, is an essential component of the gospel message. "By the power of the Holy Spirit you can become a new person," is just as much a part of the Good News as, "Your guilt is pardoned." God is personally involved in our hearts and lives to change us. He who created us in the first place is present and active within, healing what is wrong and restoring us to righteousness. Our expectations about our ethical and moral betterment are not the result of underestimating our sinfulness. They are not merely the power of positive thinking. Rather, they are trust in the promises of God. They are a result of faith in the gospel.

## II. WHAT IMPROVEMENT INVOLVES

Ethical and moral improvement cannot be verified empirically. It is not possible for us to determine with accuracy, for example, the nature and quality of motives or the existence or condition of a person's faith. We cannot know all the internal or external forces of evil against which a person has been struggling. Consequently, when trying to evaluate someone's performance in a specific area, it is not always possible to know whether we are looking at improvement or regression.

For example, in his relations with others an individual may display frequent irritation and impatience. On the surface this may appear to be regression. However, in fact it might represent dramatic improvement. This particular individual may be struggling with a violent temper or may be under tremendous emotional pressure. For him to subdue this to mere irritation and impatience may represent a major victory of the Spirit in his life. Furthermore, God often works in very quiet and subtle ways when He is in the process of transforming someone. Variable and unknown factors (Satan, too, is often hard to detect) make precise evaluation of moral improvement impossible, not only in others but also in ourselves.

On the other hand, moral improvement is discernible to some extent. The Christian himself can detect some of the changes that God is making in his heart and life. Others can notice them too. Sometimes massive improvement takes place quickly and dramatically. In other cases it occurs on a very small scale, painfully and slowly. There are many variations, but whenever ethical and moral growth takes place, the following factors are involved.

## A. Overcoming Evil

To improve involves taking the offensive against that which once held you in bondage and which still threatens you. Peace with God leads to conflict with sin and Satan. Sin is no longer regarded as a master to be obeyed, a friend to be cultivated, or a pleasure to be savored. Rather, it is regarded for what it really is—an enemy to be stopped. One mark of moral improvement is a growing militancy, an aggressive hostility against every form of evil in and around oneself.

### 1. Recognition

As the Holy Spirit does His transforming work, the Christian becomes increasingly sensitive to evil. He becomes proficient in detecting its presence and power both in self and in others. He regularly tests his heart and life with God's law. He evaluates every idea and influence that comes his way on the basis of God's Word and with the help of the Holy Spirit. Everything that deviates from or conflicts with God's revealed will is identified as evil and, therefore, as dangerous. The morally maturing Christian develops a nose for sin the way a customs inspector develops a sense for smugglers. Often, even when he cannot pin it down specifically or explain it fully, he knows that something is wrong and that he must not be deceived by it or intimidated by it.

This should not take the form of a carpingly critical spirit or an arrogant, holier-than-thou attitude toward other people. Unfortunately, such characteristics are often discerned in Christians who wish to be morally earnest. These manifestations represent not improvement but distortion, a very obnoxious kind of lovelessness. One is reminded of the moral snobbishness of the Pharisees rather than the compassionate manner in which Jesus identified evil in other people.

This growing awareness of evil should not degenerate into morbid fear of evil, or obsessive preoccupation with it. What we need and will experience, as the Spirit helps us to advance, is a realistic understanding of the pervasiveness and subtlety of sin. We will also learn a very healthy respect for its power. There is no way to improve ethically or morally apart from this developing ability to recognize sin.

### 2. Resistance

The purpose of recognizing evil is to be in a position to resist it. Evil does not dissolve when detected. It must be actively opposed, met in combat as if it were an armed enemy attacking from without, or a saboteur trying to destroy from within. Improvement is taking place when the Christian sets himself against temptation and every evil force, when instead of collaborating with or surrendering to the enemy, he vigorously and consistently resists.

The offensive weapon in the battle is the sword of the Spirit, which is the Word of God (Eph. 6 and Heb. 4). Confronted by evil in self and others the Christian can condemn it with God's law, forgive it with the gospel, and hold forth the promise and opportunity of superior alternatives. The defensive weapon is the shield of faith. Because the Christian believes in Christ, he is forgiven, and strong in the Spirit. This means that he can put down this evil that he has discovered. By sharing Christ with others he can bring them to faith or build them in faith so that they, too, can take a stand against the evil that is pulling at them.

## B. Growth in Good

As the negative is subdued, the positive is cultivated. Progress consists not only in recognizing and removing the weeds, but also in nurturing the good plants. As he learns to recognize and resist evil, the morally developing Christian experiences growth toward that which is good.

### 1. Perception

The process begins with sharpening perception. The person who is improving ethically and morally will become more clearly aware of what God's will for him really is. This will take place, not through the unfolding of an innate moral sense, but rather through rational study of the issues, responsible investigation and interpretation of biblical norms, and openness to the Spirit's guidance within. Even in difficult and ambiguous cases the Chrisitan will be able to arrive at decisions and know which way he ought to go. His skill in reading God's intentions and expectations will be refined. He will gain confidence in his ability to tell right from wrong. He will not, however, be overconfident. While sure of his perception of what is good and right and true, he will not be cocksure.

### 2. Determination

If improvement is authentic, theory will be translated into practice. Determination to do this is the mark of a growing Christian. He is not content simply to know what is right and wrong. He is committed to act accordingly in his life. He is impatient with any discrepancy between principles and practice, especially in his own life. He wants to live by his ideals. This determination is more than his own will power or personal resolve. It is modification of character achieved by the Holy Spirit. It is the nature of the new person emerging and asserting himself.

### 3. Courage

Improvement requires and displays various kinds of courage. It involves the courage to act even when one's own feelings and other formidable pressures oppose the action. It involves courage to act even when the cost is very high. One can imagine the fear and reluctance Christians behind the Iron Curtain experience as they prepare to take a stand for their Lord. They may be afraid of the consequences to themselves and their loved ones.

Friends and family may express their anxieties and plead with them to be silent. However, growing numbers are demonstrating the courage to take a stand despite these dangers and pressures.

Another form of courage which typifies the morally maturing Christian is the courage to act even when one is not perfectly confident that the decision is correct. With experience and study we discover that many moral issues are frought with ambiguities and uncertainties. Even after we have analyzed, consulted, studied, and prayed, there will be instances in which we are not positive what the Lord's will for us is in that situation. In such cases the Christian who is making ethical and moral progress will not be afraid to act. He will have the courage to do what appears best—because not to act is also a decision, and at times may be even more disastrous than doing something that is not clearly correct. The ground of this courage is not reckless bravado, but the realization that the Christian lives in the forgiveness of sins. He can dare to risk ethical and moral errors, not because God is unconcerned about wrongs which Christians do with good intentions, but because He pardons for the sake of Jesus Christ.

## III. THE CHRISTIAN SHOULD IMPROVE

Moral improvement is a necessity as well as an opportunity. Nothing in the Bible suggests that we can safely refuse to improve. On the contrary, many passages urgently charge us to work for improvement. Paul compares the Christian's efforts to improve with those of athletes training for contests (I Cor. 9:24-27). Elsewhere Paul calls upon Christians to strive for excellence (II Cor. 8:7). He encourages us to "put off your old nature... and put on the new.... Grow up in every way ... into Christ" (Eph. 4:22, 24, 15). He tells Christians to "increase and abound in love," and to do more and more of the Christian obedience that they have already exhibited (I Thess. 4).

Throughout the New Testament the Christian life is described in dynamic terms—growth, improvement, progress. Although failure and defeat are never completely eliminated as long as we are in this life, we have no reason to believe that moral stagnation or regression are acceptable and safe.

## A. Reluctance to Improve

This attitude is common, even prevalent. Many Christians are amazingly comfortable with the *status quo*. Some feel that it is their privilege as Christians not to improve, that this is part of their Christian liberty. Others feel that God does not really care whether or not we improve. "I like to sin and He likes to forgive, so improvement simply is not that important," summarizes this opinion. Still others, while acknowledging that God prefers that they improve, claim that He does not actually insist on it, and that declining to improve does no serious harm. So widespread are these views and attitudes that most of us recognize them in ourselves to various degrees. We need to review the consequences of refusal or reluctance to improve.

### 1. Dishonors God

God's purposes for us, His gifts to us, His work within us are all designed to make us better people. His investment in each one of us is enormous, and He desires to restore us to His image. His Spirit is present and active within us trying to stimulate and direct this improvement. When we resist His influence and refuse to respond to His transforming efforts, He is grieved. For us to choose to remain as we are when He endows us with the potential for Christ-likeness, when we support the growth of the old person and retard that of the new, we deeply disappoint Him.

God is also dishonored by those who claim to believe in Him but give little evidence of this in their conduct. Unbelievers, especially the militant among them, are quick to notice the contrast between the professed values and actual performance of many Christians. Some who are initially attracted to Christ and His gospel are subsequently repulsed when they discover that many Christians refuse His moral influence. "If that is all the effect He has upon His people, I want no part of Him," is their conclusion.

### 2. Deprives People

The redirection of life that constitutes moral improvement is largely for the benefit of other people. When we refuse to improve we are withholding from others some of the love and help that they need, that we owe them, and that we are in a position to give. Such refusal is in part the decision not to live for others, not to serve them, protect them, provide for them, support them, and identify with them to the extent that we could and should. It amounts to shrugging off and turning away from lonely, suffering, neglected, and condemned human beings. All of these are the losers when we refuse to improve.

### 3. Threatens Self

Ironically, the self is also harmed by its rejection of the opportunity to improve. Although the reason for refusing was to please and benefit it, the self is in fact threatened. Refusal to improve morally is refusal of God, and this is detrimental to faith. Faith is worn down and may eventually collapse in the person who consistently says no to the One who is trying to renew him. Finally he reaches the point of wondering, "How can God forgive me when I do so little in response to His love and power?" When one can no longer believe that God forgives, saving faith is gone.

Furthermore, refusal to improve invites adversity from God. He may have to take strong measures to alert us to the seriousness of our refusal. If we choose to stay with our sinful behavior patterns rather than be reformed, He may permit us to taste their bitter consequences. The person who, for example, prefers to deceive rather than to speak and act truthfully, may find himself without friends, family, and employment. By some painful experience God may try to bring him to his senses and redirect him toward improvement. Ultimately, eternal condemnation can result if, as mentioned above, faith is destroyed altogether. No one stands to lose more from a person's refusal to improve than that person himself.

## B. Results of Improvement

Improvement really matters. The Christian who gratefully employs God's love and help in order to become more like Him makes a significant impact in several areas.

### 1. Honors God

When the Christian's life improves noticeably, others will wonder why and will probably ask him. This provides a superb opportunity to glorify God, to call attention to Him and His love.

Zealous Christians sometimes press others aggressively in order to try to make them accept their witness. Often this is counterproductive, because the others are not ready for a gospel testimony.

Peter makes it clear that the best preparation for witness consists of reverent and chaste behavior, patience while suffering unjustly, and other forms of Christian moral improvement. He challenges Christians to live up to their moral potential. He also commands believers to be ready to give an answer to anyone who asks about the hope within, which is the source of the change (I Peter 2). Improvement stimulates interest in the gospel. Jesus compares the good works of His followers to light which points to the Father (Matt. 5:16). God is noticed and praised as a result of our improvement.

### 2. Benefits Others

To improve ethically and morally is to become a more useful person, one who lives more fully for God and for others. Whenever a Christian helps others become more aware of God and His redemptive love he meets their most basic need. As a Christian becomes more sensitive and loving to other people, he will discover any number of new ways to encourage and heal them. The growing Christian is as creative at serving others as he is eager and sincere. One individual acting in love, developing and expressing Christian personhood, can ameliorate human misery to an astonishing degree and can initiate a chain reaction of good which spreads far and wide.

One contemporary example, which could be multiplied many times, is Mother Theresa of Calcutta. Sent as a young Roman Catholic nun to work among the people of India, she was appalled at the conditions there. Many people were dying in the streets each day alone and unattended, and many infants were abandoned by their poverty-stricken parents. Largely alone, Mother Theresa began a ministry of love and care in Christ's name to these people with whom no one else would bother. Her example and appeals generated growing interest and support. Today, after decades of Christ-like service, she has been joined by a small army of workers, and she heads a network of welfare agencies. Her purpose is to do something beautiful for God by a growing devotion to people who need it most. She has succeeded remarkably, and the same possibility faces every Christian.

### 3. Fulfills and Rewards Self

Although we do not seek to serve ourselves by moral effort and improvement, this does, in fact, occur. In order to live more fully for God and other people we must draw heavily upon His power and love. This, inevitably, is an uplifting experience in which we discover His reality and faithfulness in a meaningful, personal way.

In addition, we discover more completely who we are and what we will ultimately become. Every stage of moral improvement is a foretaste of what we will be like when our transformation is complete in the life of the world to come. Already in this life we ordinarily enjoy temporal rewards, such as health and happiness, as a result of our increased obedience. Although for their strengthening through trial God sometimes permits the righteous to suffer, He most often reveals His approval and grace by providing them with additional blessings and joys. Most surprising of all is His promise to acknowledge and commend at the Judgment all the good that we do in His name during our lifetime. Everyone benefits when we improve morally—even ourselves.

Unfortunately, we frequently confuse cause with effect, and the consequences range from amusing to lethal. The student who attributes his poor grade to the instructor's dislike for him is probably making this mistake. In all likelihood the instructor's negativism is related to the student's lack of interest. The dislike followed rather than produced the conditions reflected in the poor grade. In the area under consideration here—moral improvement—it is also very easy to confuse cause with effect, and the consequences of doing so are extremely dangerous.

We are interested in moral improvement and actively strive for it, not in order to be saved, but because we are already saved by God's grace through Christ. We are not like aspiring athletes at a tryout doing their utmost to make the team. Rather, we are like players who have already made the team, who are established and secure in their positions. They train diligently and put their all into the game because they want to measure up to the privilege and honor which is theirs. The analogy is not completely parallel, of course, for athletes make a team on the basis of their performance and prowess. We are accepted as God's people only and completely through His mercy and generosity. However, a valid point of comparison remains. We improve, not so that we might be accepted by God, but because we already are accepted.

When we present our ethical improvement to God, it is essential that our attitude reflect a proper recognition of cause and effect. If we offer our good works to Him *as a result of the salvation* which He has graciously provided in Christ, these good works delight Him, far beyond their intrinsic worth. Even the smallest measure of improvement means a great deal to Him, if it is a response to His saving work. However, when offered up as a reason why He should forgive and save us, even the most impressive improvement will infuriate Him. He and He alone can and does save. He will not tolerate our seeking or claiming any part of the credit. Improvement is a result of salvation, *not* a cause.

# 9 CONSCIENCE

Perhaps no aspect of ethical discourse is more interesting and relevant than a consideration of conscience. Nearly all of us have functioning consciences. We are aware of them. We experience their pressures. We struggle with them. We rely on them. However, there is no general agreement about what precisely the conscience is. A variety of theories, definitions, and descriptions confronts anyone who examines what has been said and written on the subject. But despite this diversity and disagreement, there is near consensus that conscience exists and that it is indispensable. In order to come to terms with self, others, and God, an individual must have a conscience and be able to respond adequately to it.

There are some individuals in whom conscience is missing, either because it never developed or because it was destroyed in some way. The person without conscience is a serious menace to himself and to others. Although he may intellectually recognize the difference between right and wrong, there is no emotional support for the good, and no aversion for the evil. A person in this condition is comfortable, even "high," while doing something which is known to be wrong, or feels no regret about refusing to do something that is good and necessary. The technical term for such a person is "psychopath," or "sociopath." Such people constitute a threat to society and usually end up in prison or institutions for the criminally insane.

## I. NATURE AND FUNCTION OF THE CONSCIENCE

In this brief chapter an exhaustive treatment of conscience is impossible. Rather than an exposition and critique of various views and theories, this is a simple and, hopefully, a practical exposition. The goal is to deal adequately with what the Bible and evangelical theology affirm about conscience and to relate this to the daily life of the evangelical Christian. Stated concisely, the position taken here is that *conscience is the self in the process of ethical deliberation and evaluation.*

### A. Conscience Is Not External

In both technical and popular discussions, conscience is often identified with factors or persons *outside* the individual. Conscience is, for example, described as the voice of God within, or as the voice of the church, or one's parents, or society. In other words, conscience is regarded simply as the internalization of external influences. Somehow, through dependent relationships and learning situations, a person becomes conditioned to respond to the will and authority of others even when they are no longer present. Such phenomena do occur. They are related to conscience and must be considered by the ethicist, but I do not believe that any or all of these are the same as conscience. The term *conscience* is best reserved for that which is essentially *internal.*

### B. Conscience Is the Moral Self

Your conscience is not someone or something else working in or upon you. Your conscience is you, those elements of your psyche, your inner self, which deal with issues of right and wrong behavior. Your conscience is comprised of mental, emotional, and volitional components. It is you operating with these components to make moral decisions, to act upon them, and to test them for validity afterward. Your conscience is a monitor built into you which is itself part of you.

## C. Conscience Urges Compliance

In advance of any ethical decision or moral action, your conscience urges you to conform to your convictions about right and wrong. It applies spiritual and moral pressure. It leads or, if necessary, drives you toward the right and away from the wrong. If you are moving or drifting toward evil, it sounds the alarm, warning of the imminent deviation. If you are steering a true course, it reassures and reinforces. Your conscience is constantly checking on your ethical and moral responses. Even before you make your decision or begin to act upon it, your conscience supplies its strong and significant input.

## D. Conscience Sits in Judgment

Before the act, conscience tries to control and direct. Afterward it passes judgment, and it does this in a manner that is both independent and insistent. It accuses and punishes you for evil decisions and actions, often mercilessly and relentlessly. Even if you are innocent before the law of the land, even if society accepts and approves of what you did, your conscience will condemn you if *you* believe what you did is wrong. In response to the accusations of conscience, people do some remarkable things, as will be described later in this chapter.

On the other hand, conscience also acknowledges and praises you for doing what you believe is right and for avoiding what you believe is wrong. Few rewards can match the approval of one's own conscience, the sense of relief and satisfaction that comes from knowing that you have been faithful to your moral convictions. A "good" conscience is in part one which commends you. A "bad" conscience is in part one which condemns you.

## II. CONSCIENCE AND THE MORAL STANDARD

Because they are closely related, conscience and the moral standard are often confused. There is a difference. Clarity and consistency require that this distinction be observed.

## A. Conscience Applies the Moral Standard

Your moral standard is your set of beliefs and judgments about what is right and wrong to do. It is your impression of God's will, your guidelines for conduct, your ethical norms to the extent that you have worked them out. As will be explained below, your conscience does not formulate or establish these standards. Other forces and factors do that. Nor is "conscience" merely a synonym for "moral standard." Rather, your conscience is the enforcer of your moral standard. It refers you to your moral standard and attempts to persuade you to live by it.

Your moral standard may be compared with the legislative branch of government, which passes laws and decides how individual and social behavior should be regulated. Your conscience may be compared with the executive branch, which enforces the law, and the judicial branch, which determines guilt and innocence and imposes penalties for wrongdoing.

## B. The Moral Standard Is Formed by Learning, Experience, and Belief

Every human being has an inborn sense of right and wrong. This is regarded by many as a lingering vestige of the image of God, or insight into His will which God planted in people at the creation. Traditionally it has been termed the "natural knowledge of the law." Valuable and useful as it is, the natural knowledge of the law is incomplete and distorted. Much of the awareness of God's will was obliterated in people by the fall. All is limited by our human finitude and dimmed by our sinfulness. Part of our basic development as human beings has to do with the building and revision of the moral standard, our sense of right and wrong. From family, peers, society, culture, and the church, formative influences reach us and shape our moral standard.

A Christian's moral standard is, hopefully, formed and informed primarily by God's Word and Spirit. Throughout life this standard is in the process of being enlarged, reinforced, or revised. New issues rise out of the new possibilities that confront us as a result of social and technological change. We must make judgments and decisions about their moral significance in order to act responsibly concerning them. In some cases new information or improved perception make it necessary for us to change our moral standard. Your moral standard is your understanding of what you ought and ought not to do. Your conscience keeps this before you and urges you to conform to it.

## III. POTENTIALS AND LIMITATIONS

Conscience can be a major force and factor in our lives. It is capable of affecting us profoundly and of rendering us vital services. However, it also has its limitations. It can be ignored and disabled. It can also make mistakes. To expect too much of conscience is as unwise as to expect too little.

### A. Persistent, but Not Irresistible

When violated, conscience can inflict great pain and distress. It can make us uncomfortable over long periods of time, haunt and hound us for years, perhaps never relenting until we finally comply with its demands. For example, the United States government has a "Conscience Fund" to receive money from taxpayers who successfully falsified their returns, but are eventually driven by conscience to pay everything they owe. From time to time the news media report on individuals who committed crimes for which they were never apprehended. Decades later, in some cases, these individuals have turned themselves in to the authorities. Although they had evaded justice, their consciences would give them no rest.

Conscience can also act powerfully to prevent wrongdoing. I know a woman who, although elderly and severely arthritic, chose to live in poverty rather than accept an insurance settlement which her conscience recognized as fraudulent. Her husband was killed in a collision with an automobile driven by a person who was drunk. It happened at an intersection controlled by a stop light. She was the only passenger, and there were no other witnesses. Because the other driver was heavily intoxicated at the time of the accident, everyone—the police, the insurance company, even the driver himself—assumed that he had gone through the red light and caused the accident. The insurance company was ready to make a large financial settlement, which the woman needed, for her husband was her only source of income. However, she knew beyond all doubt that her husband, and not the drunken driver, had gone against the red light. Her lawyer, friends, and family pleaded with her not to divulge this, but her conscience protested. Drunk or not, the other driver had not caused the accident and should not be blamed for it. She was not entitled to the settlement under the circumstances and would not seek or accept it. As a consequence she had to live on a meager welfare allotment for the rest of her life. Conscience is an awesome force with which to reckon.

However, conscience is not irresistible or invincible. It can be ignored or defied. If suppressed often enough in a given area, it may eventually stop complaining, that is, it may become calloused or totally inoperative in that area. If violated often enough in many areas, the conscience can be destroyed, along with faith itself. "Some men have not listened to their conscience and have made a ruin of their faith" (I Tim. 1:19, TEV).

The gradual desensitization of the conscience is not an uncommon experience, even among Christians. Many report that the first time they committed a certain sinful act, their conscience reacted sharply with acute distress and guilt. The next time they did it, the reaction of conscience was noticeably diminished. After numerous repetitions of the act, the conscience no longer responded at all. Whether the act is one of dishonesty, cruelty, sexual immorality, or blasphemy, the conscience can eventually be silenced.

Unfortunately, there are some "educational" or "therapeutic" experiences which are deliberately designed to have this effect. For example, some "human sexuality workshops" expose participants to motion pictures depicting a wide variety of explicit, immoral sexual activity, followed by discussions with persons who admit to being involved in this activity. The purpose is to relieve participants of their "hang-ups," that is to say, the tendency of their conscience to recognize and reject these behaviors as evil. Viewing enough of this material has an effect similar to doing it oneself. It stills the conscience in this area. First of all, it removes objections regarding the involvement of others in these behaviors and eventually regarding one's own involvement.

These observations are not intended as a blanket condemnation of sex education or sexual therapy, both of which can be done in a morally sound manner, and which need to be done in many cases. Rather, what is described and condemned here is calculated efforts to disarm consciences, to render them helpless against morally harmful stimuli.

## B. Consistent, but not Infallible

A healthy conscience is reliable in the sense that it almost always points in the same direction, like a good compass. It points to *your* moral standard. Although it may and should undergo constant review and a certain amount of revision, your moral standard remains essentially the same today as it was yesterday. Tomorrow and in the years to come that standard will probably not differ markedly from what it is now. With great consistency your conscience, if it is functioning properly, will direct you to that standard when you are trying to make up your mind about what you ought to do.

Conscience is not soft, and it is not easily fooled. It will not readily succumb to rationalization, whether from you or from someone else. Conscience often refuses to be swayed even by strong popular opinion or by the serious dangers which you may encounter if you follow its guidance. Stubbornly and steadily, conscience points in the direction that your moral standard indicates, like the needle of a compass holding firmly to magnetic north.

Reliable is not the same as infallible. Though consistent and reliable, the conscience can make mistakes simply because the moral standard to which it refers is not always correct. Your moral standard may be misinformed in some areas. From various sources you may have received the impression that certain behaviors are sinful even though God, in fact, approves of them. And, of course, the reverse also happens. Paul refers to Christians who sincerely believed that it was sinful to eat meat (Rom. 14). Elsewhere Scripture refers to Christians whose moral standard has accommodated itself to adultery. Twentieth-century moral standards are no less susceptible to error. "Let your conscience be your guide" is valid only if these limitations are kept in mind.

## IV. GOD'S MINISTRY TO THE CONSCIENCE

As God relates to us and communicates with us, He gives special attention to our conscience. Above all He is eager to make an impact in the very depth of our inner being, in this part of us that is involved in moral decisions and evaluation. Since His ultimate purpose is not only to rescue us from the consequences of corruption, but also to rehabilitate us into new people, it is necessary for Him to deal directly and decisively with the monitor of our behavior. Conscience serves as a link between His will and ours.

### A. God Addresses the Conscience with both Law and Gospel

This is the heart of God's message whenever He communicates with us. Whatever else He might have to say, whatever else we might want to hear, He always connects it with these key elements of His revelation. We need both law and gospel. Neither can accomplish His purpose alone.

With the law, God reinforces the accusations of conscience. When we violate conscience, and conscience in turn accuses us, God's law usually supports and even intensifies that accusation. Through His law, God warns us that our disobedience is every bit as serious and threatening as conscience indicates, perhaps worse. The unsettling discovery to which He leads us through the message of the law is that we must answer not only to an angry conscience, but also to an angry God. This is, of course, very bad news. We would rather not hear it, but we must, if we are to be helped. Until the full seriousness of our condition is apparent to us and has registered clearly on our minds and feelings, we are unprepared for any positive and supportive word from God.

God speaks His accusing and condemning word of law in a variety of ways. It may reach us through a penetrating sermon, through a word of admonition or rebuke from a fellow Christian, through a passage of Scripture read or remembered. Sometimes God speaks law to us through actions as well as words. By a shattering adversity He may jolt us into the realization that we have angered Him with our sins.

Not every adversity has this significance. Frequently, God uses sorrow and trouble simply to draw us closer to Himself, to strengthen our faith through testing. We must read the language of adversity carefully and honestly. To the question, "What have I done to deserve this?" the answer is always, "Plenty!" However, if we are already aware of our sin and guilt and sincerely sorry for it, God does not aim His law at us either in the form of word or adversity. The thoroughly awakened and terrified conscience is already responding to His law, and God does not assault it with still more law.

However, in many if not most cases, our conscience is falsely secure and insensitive, or reacting in a weak and apathetic way to the presence of sin. This means that conscience must be aroused and its accusations amplified. It is in such cases that God tries to get at our conscience with the message of His law in whatever form is most likely to be effective.

Troubling people's consciences is not God's favorite pastime. His primary purpose and chief delight is in relieving the pangs of conscience with the Good News of forgiveness in Jesus Christ. Accusing our conscience with the law is His strange and foreign work. Comforting conscience with the gospel is His proper and characteristic work. He disturbs and distresses us with the law because He must—our welfare, as well as His justice and holiness, require it. He heals and pardons with the gospel because He wants to. His dominant characteristic and most compelling impulse is to love and to help us.

Law and gospel are both authentic and essential expressions of His will, but they are not equally important. The law is there for the sake of the gospel, but not *vice versa*. The gospel is preeminent. More than anything else, God wants to minister to our conscience with the gospel, to apply His Word of pardon, acceptance, and hope when conscience accuses us.

Often we seek relief in other ways. We ventilate our guilt feelings, tell others about what is bothering us, and this can help. It is consoling to share deep feelings of any kind with other human beings and to experience their interest and acceptance. Neurotic or misplaced guilt may require psychotherapy. Or, we may try to compensate for our wrongdoing by virtuous and generous behavior. By doing something that is good and right, we hope to diminish the accusations of conscience over the wrongs that we have done. Or we may make excuses. We may try to explain to ourselves and others why what we did was really not all that bad, or why it was, in fact, unavoidable. Or we may simply try to escape conscience by keeping our minds and time occupied with other things. In varying degrees, these and similar mechanisms may provide some temporary and superficial relief.

However, since God ultimately is the victim of every sin, we need His Word of forgiveness above all. Only He can deal effectively with the conscience that is complaining about real and condemning sins. This He does in the gospel. For Christ's sake He offers pardon for any and all sins. None is too serious or too disgusting for Him to handle. The Good News is the assurance that Jesus died for all sins and can release us from their guilt, even those sins which bother us most. Having presented our sins to Him and pleaded guilty for them, we can be confident that, as far as He is concerned, our record is clean and, because of this, our conscience can also be at rest.

There are cases in which conscience continues to accuse and condemn even after the gospel has been applied. This condition might be evidence of insincere confession, a pretense of sorrow for sin combined with a secret determination to continue in it. Or it might reflect a weak and wavering faith, lack of confidence in Christ's willingness or ability to forgive. In any case, the conscience that refuses to accept the comfort of the gospel, and continues to torment a person despite God's expressions of love and pardon, has become the voice and instrument of the devil. It is misled and misleading and should be rejected instead of heeded.

## B. Correcting and Building the Moral Standard

As has already been stated, it is extremely important that the moral standard which conscience enforces be valid and accurate. Since sources other than God's Word supply input to our moral standard and help to shape it, and since our moral standard may be in error, we need God's ongoing guidance and clarification through the Word. We should review and examine our moral standard again and again in the light of Scripture in order to evaluate and correct it.

It may take time for conscience to adjust to some new or revised item in the moral standard. Intellectually, a person may accept a changed value, but emotionally he may balk at the change, at least for a while. For example, after careful study and reflection a Christian may repudiate long-standing racist attitudes. However, initially conscience may continue to tolerate them or fail to detect them. Only gradually does it become acquainted with and responsive to the changed standard. During this transitional period it may require special effort and attention on the part of the Christian to live by the revised standard.

For all practical purposes, the Christian responds to the moral standard as to the voice of God. The moral standard to which conscience refers contains our best understanding of God's will for our lives, our clearest conviction of what He wants us to do and to avoid. To act against our perception of God's will is, in effect, a personal revolt against God Himself. He knows when we intend to disobey, and He reacts against that rebellious spirit even in cases when our moral standard was incorrect and the action itself was not wrong.

"But if he has doubts about what he eats, God condemns him when he eats it, because his action is not based on faith. And anything that is not based on faith is sin" (Rom. 14:23, TEV). In short, although conscience and the moral standard are fallible and have their limitations, they are authoritative and essential factors in the moral life.

# 10 PROCESS

We have considered some of the most important forces and factors with which the Christian must come to terms as he tries to decide and do what is right. They are: corruption, motivation, norms, forms, reason, resources, failure, improvement, and conscience. We have explored these items individually and noted some of the ways in which they relate to one another.

At this point we need a process, an orderly and systematic method which puts these things together and makes an operable ethical system. In this chapter such a process is described. It consists of a conventional problem-solving method into which the basic components of Christian ethics have been inserted. The form into which this process has been integrated is a step-by-step operation, concrete and practical in nature, by which the serious Christian can make the kinds of analysis and application that the ethical task requires.

This process is offered with the conviction that it is both sound and effective, that it is a useful way to work through difficult and confusing moral issues. It is not, however, the only way; other approaches may be equally valid and workable. God has nowhere revealed a complete ethical process, though He has supplied us with necessary truths about Himself and ourselves. In Christian liberty and on the basis of "sanctified" common sense, we are to develop or adapt an ethical method which incorporates these truths and which works satisfactorily for us.

A process of this kind is necessary only for exceptionally complex and ambiguous ethical questions. For the vast majority of our ethical decisions, the detailed or involved process described below is unnecessary. We have a moral standard, that is, clear and confident convictions about right and wrong, in most areas of life. In at least nine out of ten ethical decisions conscience applies the moral standard, and no further thought or research is necessary. We know almost reflexively what we ought to do or avoid from the moral standard. Doing what we believe is right may not always be easy, but knowing what is right is quite automatic in most cases, as the conscience reads and interprets the moral standard.

However, in some situations we do not know clearly and readily what we ought to do. We are confronted by alternatives about which Scripture does not speak explicitly or with finality. Our moral standard is not formed or informed about the matter. We are confused by conflicting views and values which others express. We must cross new and uncharted territory. Although this may happen only in a minority of cases, it does happen. When it does, we need a process, an organized method of exploring the question and determining God's will.

In those rare instances we need such a process urgently. Otherwise we may act impulsively or intuitively, which is simply unwise. Impulses and intuition are too easily swayed by the worst elements in and around us. To act responsibly we need to utilize the best available information and guidance, and this almost inevitably involves a process.

### 1. Seek the Spirit's Guidance and Strength

As has been stated, evangelical ethics is, above all, ethics of the Holy Spirit. In the struggle to arrive at a perception of right and wrong in a confusing situation, we have more to go on than some written guidelines and our own judgment. We have a Person, a living, loving, divine Person—the Holy Spirit. He is present with us in the struggle, communicating, influencing, and encouraging. Jesus refers to Him as the Counselor who will lead us into all truth.

It is not just a pious platitude that Christian ethical reflection must begin, continue, and end with the Holy Spirit. As we go about the task of investigating, weighing, and deciding, we should be aware of the Spirit's presence. We should specifically request His involvement, confessing our dependence upon Him. In Scripture He offers us His help. He promises to listen and respond to our requests for spiritual and moral assistance of any kind. We should take Him at His Word and act on the basis of His promises. Throughout each step of the process we should review in prayer with Him all the input that we receive from outside sources as well as our own thoughts and insights. We should keep in close and continuous contact with Him, make Him our partner in the process. No other factor is more vital to wise and true ethical response than the presence and influence of the Spirit.

The Spirit is also an indispensable source of strength. To do what we recognize as God's will always requires more moral strength than we possess. In many cases it requires extraordinary courage, determination, and selflessness. For this, too, we should be reaching out to the Holy Spirit consciously and consistently. We should admit our weakness and rely confidently on Him to provide the needed strength. Only what we do by His power and guidance can be considered good, in the strictest sense of the word. If we neglect this first step—involving the Spirit—the rest of the process is certain to break down.

### 2. Analyze and Research the Issue

The second step consists of rational inquiry, in which we gather information about the problem at hand and interpret it to the best of our ability. It includes taking advantage of the study and experience of others by reading what they have written on the subject or by consulting them. Our purpose in this step is to try to understand the issue or problem as clearly as possible, to become aware of its extent, complexities, implications, as well as the various possibilities and alternatives related to it. Not only the issue in general but also our particular situation must be investigated. We should also try to determine how one's individuality, as well as that of others who are involved, affects the moral character of the issue.

A serious difficulty in carrying out this step is the overwhelming mass of material which is available on many issues with which we must deal. Information, interpretations, opinions, conclusions—many of which are divergent or even conflicting—are there in great profusion, bidding for our attention and acceptance. Consequently, we must learn how to select carefully and wisely among the available materials. Since we cannot explore everything, we must become skilled in determining in advance which sources are likely to be most reliable and useful. Such skill is, hopefully, gained in the course of formal education. However, it may also be acquired by experience and in informal learning situations.

Another essential skill in analyzing and researching a moral issue is the ability to distinguish between facts, opinions, and interpretations. Usually these are intermingled in the reports and comments on moral issues which we study. They need to be distinguished and sorted out, for they have different kinds of authority and value. Furthermore, we need to be able to uncover the presuppositions and biases of the persons whose work we consider, and determine how these affect their work.

Frequently, when trying to understand an unfamiliar area about which you have to make an ethical decision, it is necessary to rely on a knowledgeable and experienced person who can guide you. Such a person can direct you to the most relevant and accurate information, can help you to recognize some of the key questions, and can serve as a sounding board for your ideas and conclusions as they are formed.

In choosing such a person, it is extremely important to know his beliefs and values. Despite claims which are often made to the contrary, these do affect a counselor's selection and interpretation of data, as well as his recommendations. Without realizing that it is happening, a counselee's or a student's moral standard will often be revised into that of the counselor or teacher. Evangelical Christians who wish to retain their belief and value systems will do well to rely for expert help on other evangelical Christians. (On the other hand, it is also advisable to get a viewpoint different from one's own. Evangelical Christians have no monopoly on expertise or truth. The limitations of one's own moral tradition are often more obvious to the outsider than to the insider.)

Very early in the ethical process it is necessary to come to an adequate understanding of the issue, through research and rational analysis. In the absence of good information and interpretation about the problem, one may make poor decisions and take harmful courses of action, with the very best of intentions.

A dramatic example of this is the kind of assistance given to poor and underdeveloped nations after World War II. Confronted by widespread infectious diseases among the people of these countries, the United States and other "advanced" nations supplied them with large quantities of antibiotic medicines, thus saving millions of lives. What we did not realize, because of inadequate research, was that these nations were woefully undersupplied with food. By saving many lives with medicine, we had in fact merely increased the number of those who would die of starvation. Reducing the death rate without proportionately increasing the food supply was not exactly a kindness. Valid moral decisions must be based on adequate information and insight, and this requires analysis and research.

### 3. Come to Terms with Corruption in Self and Others

The presence and power of sin intrudes prominently into the decision-making process. We need to be aware of this and to have a healthy respect for it. Although the guilt of our sin is completely forgiven through faith in Jesus Christ, the power of sin is still active within us, confusing and misleading. In ways that are often very subtle and difficult to discern, the power of sin tries to make good seem evil and evil good. The best, wisest, and most pious Christian persons whom we consult are also sinful, capable of misleading and of being mislead. As ideas and views are forming about a moral issue, as information and influence come our way from other people, we must be willing to ask some hard and embarassing questions: In what way and to what extent may this be twisted, distorted by sin, corrupt, of the devil?

One important way to test an idea, view, or value for corruption is to compare it, in presupposition, implication, and substance, with God's revealed will in the law. The problem is that many of the most troublesome issues which we confront are dealt with only indirectly or obliquely in Scripture. However, by careful study and inference we will be able to discover areas of contact and similarity. We will be able to detect or at least to sense deviation from God's will.

In addition to the written Word of Scripture with which to test for corruption, we also have the Holy Spirit within. He illuminates and judges the components of moral decisions as they are forming. As we deal with information and views about moral issues, we should submit them to Him in prayer and contemplation, asking Him to expose and condemn whatever is wrong. Scripture and the Spirit keep us alert to the presence of corruption and thus able to minimize its influence.

### 4. Identify, Interpret, and Apply Biblical Norms

Discovering biblical norms can be very challenging. In this part of the process we are trying to find guidance in the Bible for issues which are not discussed there directly or in detail. We are working with issues and points of interpretation about which there may be no clear consensus even among sensitive, committed, and informed evangelical Christians. To identify, interpret, and apply biblical norms under these circumstances is a delicate and somewhat tenuous operation. However, it must be undertaken. Otherwise, instead of depending primarily on God for guidance, we will be depending on ourselves or other equally limited and corrupt human beings, and that would be dangerous.

What kind of biblical norms can we hope to find in cases like this? Perhaps the best way to describe them is to say that although they may be sufficient and even convincing, they are not absolute.

As may be recalled from chapter 3, biblical ethical norms are, first of all, a model of Christian personhood. By a large number of biblical commands and moral examples regarding many areas of life, God creates in us a sense or a feel of His will. On the basis of what He has revealed in these areas, we can often predict quite accurately what His will is also in those areas not discussed specifically in Scripture.

Furthermore, we can arrive at valid moral principles and rules. This requires not only a sensitive, inferential interpretation of relevant Scripture, but also careful analysis of the context of the moral issue. *Principles* are general guidelines ("Conserve nonrenewable energy resources"). *Rules* are more specific ("Keep the thermostat at 65 degrees or lower"). If we have examined both Scripture and the moral issue diligently and have been open to the Spirit's guidance, we will emerge with direction from God which is an adequate basis for action.

The level of certainty may vary. On one issue we may come to a very clear and confident conviction about what the will of God is. On another we may be less sure that we have perceived God's will accurately. On still another we may have serious questions about the correctness of our moral judgment. In the latter case, one would prefer not to have to act, in order to wait for greater clarification and confidence, but that is not always possible. Often we must act even in the face of ethical and moral uncertainty. God has not promised always to lead us to absolute ethical norms, but He has promised direction sufficient to enable us to live responsibly in this confusing and sinful world. More important, He promises grace to cover the ethical and moral mistakes which we inevitably make, no matter how conscientiously we may try to avoid them.

The element of uncertainty in these ethical norms should be reflected in the way that we use them. Since God has not spoken explicitly and unequivocally on these issues, we cannot be dogmatic about them. We may and must be sure enough to decide and act ourselves. We may feel confident enough to try to persuade others to accept and live by these norms, too. However, we cannot demand that others accept our perception of God's will in these ambiguous areas. We must respect the right and responsibility of others to identify and formulate ethical norms for themselves, and to come to conclusions different form our own.

Furthermore, we should be willing to consider the ethical views of those who disagree with us; we should examine the Scriptural and factual bases of their views and compare them with our own. The element of uncertainty makes an attitude of humility and openness on our part most appropriate. Nevertheless, the conclusion to which we have come by our own prayer, study, and reflection is authoritative and binding for us until and unless are convinced differently from Scripture or other valid sources.

In this connection it may be well to restate some basic guidelines for interpreting biblical ethical norms. These were discussed more fully in chapter 5: (1) New Testament material has precedence over Old Testament material. (2) Clear imperatives have more authority than moral examples. (3) Clear imperatives have more authority than directives inferred from doctrines. (4) Historically and culturally conditioned commands must be distinguished from those which are binding for all times. (5) Ethical norms should be based on at least several clear passages of Scripture.

Here, as in the previous step of the process, the assistance of a knowledgeable and experienced person can be invaluable. Many Christians need help locating and understanding the biblical material which speaks to the moral issue which they are pondering. They also need help selecting works which comment on these Scripture passages. All Christians can benefit from ethical discussion with other competent Christians as they are searching out God's will. Such discussion provides them with the opportunity to clarify and test the validity of their own position. Although we must all, ultimately, make our own ethical decisions, it is only prudent to take advantage of the best available counsel and aid.

### 5. Examine, Correct, and Strengthen Motives

Motives can make or break an ethical decision. They profoundly affect the quality of a moral action. As a critical factor in the process, they require close scrutiny, delicate adjustment, and solid support.

To properly investigate and evaluate our own motives we must be not only candid but even downright suspicious. We have to ask some deep and unsettling questions: What is moving me as I make this decision or take this course or action? Are my professed reasons the real reasons? Or are they just a cover for other, less admirable motives which I do not like to admit even to myself? Am I really most concerned to honor God and help people and only secondarily to please or serve myself? To what extent are my motives mixed, that is, permeated with selfish, loveless, godless impulses? To what extent is the devil moving me, rather than God?

Questions like these inevitably turn up evidences of sinfulness. But this does not mean that they reveal *only* sinfulness. The Holy Spirit and the new person are also alive and effective within us, generating authentic motivation. However, mingled with and often overshadowing these are unworthy motives originating from the old person and the enemy. Once we face up to these corrupt motives, God forgives and counteracts them.

In addition, God reinforces the proper motivation which grows out of faith, love, and self-acceptance. He does this by presenting Christ to us in the gospel, by offering us love, reconciliation, and transformation through Him along with a new vision of what we can become. Along with Christ God gives us the Holy Spirit, who penetrates the depths of our being, adjusting, purifying, and energizing us. In the final analysis God is not satisfied only to be our motivator; He also wants to be our chief motive. By honest probing into our motives, we can facilitate His functioning in this way.

### 6. Establish Suitable Goals

A goal is something we hope to accomplish through a specific course of action. Ordinarily it involves a change which we intend to make in a given situation. Our goal should be consistent with and expressive of the directive we arrive at as we identify, interpret, and apply biblical norms. In fact, the goal is the concrete application of that directive or norm.

Several examples may clarify both the relation and the distinction between norms and goals. Suppose that the problem or issue with which you are dealing is an unhappy and disappointing marriage. Your question is: What should I do about this marriage? What does God want me to do? First, you must identify the relevant biblical norms according to the procedure described in step four. Your reading of that norm might be: cherish, preserve, and improve your marriage. However, in order to follow that norm with any degree of success, you must first translate it into concrete and practical changes that you propose to make in your marriage to follow God's will. Such steps might be: restore communication with my spouse; revive affection and respect; eliminate causes of tension. Goals are proposed revisions in attitude and behavior derived from biblical norms.

Another example, this time related to a social issue, also illustrates how goals may be derived from norms. An urgent need which should be stabbing the conscience of every Christian in the Western world is that of hunger. What should we do about the growing multitudes in underdeveloped nations who are starving? If we listen to Scripture on this issue, we will hear the norm loud and clear: Feed the hungry; get help to them; assume responsibility for them. However, this is still very general and, consequently, vague. To give focus and clarity to our response, we must translate the biblical norm and directive into a definite and manageable thesis. This may involve addressing only one or two aspects of the problem. With regard to world hunger, our goal might be to get food to starving Africans as soon as possible, or do something to avert future famines there, or both. We are far more likely to respond and to respond effectively to a moral issue if we formulate a definite goal on the basis of the biblical norm.

To be suitable, a goal must not only be specific and consistent with God's will, it must also be feasible and attainable. It must hold some realistic promise of being accomplished. Although it is healthy and stimulating to elevate our sights and establish lofty and challenging goals, it is counterproductive to set them too high. In deciding what we ought to do, we must express this in terms of what we are able to do. As Christians we have good reasons for being optimistic to the point of daring, because we are assured of God's own involvement and support in the good that we undertake in His name. However, this should not be construed as encouragement for reckless and unreachable goals.

A critical factor in goal setting is assessment of probable consequences. As we determine the target of our moral effort, we should try to anticipate both the short- and long-range results of the goals under consideration. New problems can be hidden in many proposed solutions. The case mentioned in step two, above, is a tragic example of this. The laudable purpose of healing disease and relieving the suffering connected with it eventually created a larger and even more pathetic problem—mass starvation.

Conversely, the selection of a worthy long-term goal may have painful immediate consequences. A friend of mine was born deaf. His parents decided that they ought to prepare him to function as much as possible like a hearing person. This meant that he was not permitted to learn sign language or associate with the deaf community. Rather, he was forced to become proficient at lip-reading and speaking, in order to get along in the hearing community. This involved a considerable amount of frustration and pain in early childhood. However, he became so proficient at lip-reading and speaking that he was able to complete conventional schooling through the high school level with good grades. He was able to operate comfortably in the hearing community, to hold a job which, ordinarily, only a hearing person could hold. Some people did not even realize that he was deaf. The goal which his parents selected was ethical as well as educational. They wanted to do what would be best for him. They selected a goal on the basis on long- rather than short-range consequences, and their judgment appears to have been sound.

## 7. *Determine and Employ Appropriate Means*

Once we have arrived at a suitable goal, we must devise a way to reach it. Usually there are a number of possibilities. In selecting a means, the Christian is concerned that the means itself be moral, consistent with and expressive of God's will. No matter how worthy the goal, it is wrong to attempt to reach it by evil means. *The end does not justify the means.* For example, it would not be right or appropriate to provide food for victims of famine by means of lying, cheating, stealing, killing, and so on. In an extreme case it might be *necessary* to resort to an evil means, but the means would still be evil.

This raises the issue of what is sometimes called "the principle of the lesser evil." In this corrupt and complicated world, we do not always have a choice between good and evil alternatives. Sometimes all the alternatives appear to contain clear and serious evil. For example, in order to save someone from a murderous assailant, we may lie about that person's whereabouts. Under such circumstances is the lie good and right?

Some ethicists would say yes. Because it was done to help and protect someone in great danger, the lie in this case was not only permissible but actually good. However, Christians who believe in absolute biblical ethical norms say no. They claim that lying is always a sin, even when done in a desperate situation and in order to avert suffering or death. The person who tells a lie even under these circumstances must humbly bow under the judgment of God's law on account of it and cast himself on God's mercy in Christ.

Faced with a moral dilemma in which we must choose among several evils, we select the alternative which is least evil. However, in so doing we must not assume that we or the action are justified because it was the lesser evil. If we are justified, it is only because we acknowledge it penitently as sin and accept God's pardon for the sake of Jesus' sacrifice.

To be appropriate, a means, like a goal, must also be feasible. It must be workable, sensible, likely to succeed. There is no virtue in setting off on some grandiose scheme that is certain to fail. Ethical and moral responsibility exclude empty heroics. Sober, rational investigation and analysis, together with careful planning and preparation, can lead to the adoption of feasible means.

The goals mentioned above for improving a troubled marriage might be attained through a variety of means. Communication might be facilitated and tension relieved by a skilled and sensitive counselor, or by a marriage enrichment experience. A changed lifestyle which enables the spouses to spend more time together may rekindle closeness. Reducing expenditures may relieve tension over financial problems. More frequent and imaginative expressions of affection may revive love and passion. Avoidance of hurtful and offensive behavior and faithful observance of commitments may restore trust and respect.

Appropriate means for feeding the hungry of the world might be lowering one's standard of living and contributing the money thus saved to the hungry. Or it might be to study agriculture, become an expert in food production, move to some famine-plagued area, and there try to avert future famines. Or it might be to write a book or play to awaken the consciences of others to the needs of starving people and to elicit a supporting response from them.

Obviously, in the selection of means, one's own abilities, resources, opportunities, responsibilities, and roles play a decisive part. The concept of Christian vocation is relevant at this point. God ordinarily calls us to serve Him and other people in our existing relationships and roles. Occasionally He calls individuals to leave their present context to serve in a new place and a new way, but that is the exception. Before looking outside our present situation for means with which to respond to a moral challenge, we should explore the opportunities within that situation.

For example, as a professor of theology, I can probably do far more to alleviate world hunger by teaching, speaking, and writing on the subject than by trying to show people elsewhere how to increase their food production. My financial contributions are far more valuable than my personal presence and involvement in a famine area. However, if I were a young person choosing a career, especially if I had an interest in and aptitude for agricultural science, I might feel called by God to choose a different means of trying to do something about world hunger.

### 8. Draw Upon Spiritual and Moral Resources

In order to make good ethical decisions and then live by them, we need to be spiritually and morally strong. This will happen only if we use the resources that God has provided, the media through which He conveys His guidance and power to us. Especially when working through a difficult moral issue, we need to draw heavily upon His Word and sacrament and make much use of prayer.

Unfortunately, the opposite often happens. We become so preoccupied with the issue before us that we are distracted from God and the help that He makes available. We become so aware of the problem and anxious about it that we overlook solutions close at hand. Every ethical decision, expecially one which troubles and confuses, is an invitation from God to turn to Him and to draw on the resources which He provides.

In addition to God's Word, the Lord's Supper, and prayer, the fellowship of His people is a vital spiritual and moral resource. Not in isolation, but in the community of believers, we should discuss, explore, and resolve our ethical problems. We should test our values. views, and conclusions against those of other informed and experienced Christians. We can find inspiration and encouragement in the moral example of our brothers and sisters in the faith. We can count on them for correction and admonition when we need it. To a significant degree our moral and spiritual strength depends on our use of these resources.

## 9. Conduct Adequate Evaluation

Rarely do we progress or improve in any area without some kind of evaluation. Ideally this will include constructive criticism from others as well as self-evaluation. In order to do better we must become aware of our mistakes so that we can avoid them in the future. We also need to know what we are doing that is correct so that we can reinforce these areas of strength and build upon them. An athlete will listen to his coach and his teammates. He will also study his own performance at practice, during a game, or on film.

Our ethical performance, too, requires evaluation. After we have made a decision and acted upon it, we should review what has happened and reflect upon it. Was it wise, honest, effective? Where were our reasoning and interpretation faulty? Where were they sound? Where were we misinformed? Where were we accurately informed? At what points, if any, were we rationalizing? What aided or interfered with the implementation of the decision? What did we do that was valid and responsible? What were the consequences? How accurately did we anticipate them?

The purpose of evaluation is not to grieve over our mistakes or gloat over our successes, but rather to learn from experience.

### 10. Rely on God's Forgiveness

Whether the evaluation is positive or negative, what we need more than anything else in the world is God's forgiveness. Even when we make correct decisions and act upon them conscientiously, our performance is still inadequate, acceptable to God only because of His mercy in Christ. However, in many cases we make very bad decisions or fail to act upon our good decisions. Because of this we are guilty before God and under His judgments. Only through the forgiveness of sins can we or our ethical performance stand before Him. We can be sure that God accepts us not because we are ethically brilliant or morally successful, but rather because His Son died for us.

\* \* \*

It is fitting that we conclude on this gospel note. As we stated at the beginning, an evangelical ethic is centered in the gospel of God's forgiving love in Jesus Christ. For direction, for the power to change, as well as for making our performance acceptable, we rely upon Him. He is not only our Savior from sin but also our model and motive for new personhood. In the ethical task we do employ other gifts of God beside the gospel—the law and human reason, for example. However, they are always auxiliary and subordinate to the gospel. The gospel is the mainspring of the Christian life, as well as the object of saving faith.

# FOR FURTHER READING

George A. Chauncey, *Decisions! Decisions!* (Richmond, Va: John Knox Press, 1972). A useful and delightful little book which discusses and illustrates different types of ethical reasoning.

David Field, *Taking Sides* (Downers Grove, Ill: InterVarsity Press, 1975). A brief but helpful attempt to apply biblical principles to some contemporary moral issues, such as ecology, abortion, divorce, work, and race.

George W. Forell, *Ethics of Decision: An Introduction to Christian Ethics* (Philadelphia: Fortress Press, 1955). Interesting and understandable, but by no means simplistic.

Carl F. Henry, editor, *Baker's Dictionary of Christian Ethics* (Grand Rapids, Mich: Baker Book House, 1973). A splendid reference work. Articles on a wide variety of ethical terms and topics by competent evangelical scholars.

———*Christian Personal Ethics* (Grand Rapids, Mich: Baker Book House, 1957). A masterful exposition by a distinguished evangelical theologian-philosopher. Affirms a clear biblical ethic over against both ancient and modern alternatives. Broad in scope, learned, challenging.

Adolph Koeberle, *The Quest for Holiness: A Biblical, Historical and Systematic Investigation.* John C. Mattees, translator (Minneapolis: Augsburg Publishing House, 1936). In my judgment the most significant and helpful discussion in English of the relationship between justification and sanctification, the theological pivot of all ethical discourse. Difficult, but worth the effort.

C. S. Lewis, *Christian Behavior*, printed with several other works in *Mere Christianity,* revised and enlarged edition (New York: Macmillian Co., 1960). A basic but penetrating introduction to Christian ethics by the eminent British apologist. Clear, engaging, written for the non-expert.

James B. Nelson, *Human Medicine: Ethical Perspectives on New Medical Issues* (Minneapolis: Augsburg Publishing House, 1973). An informative and provocative presentation by a leading authority. Discussion of difficult issues in this expanding field with a range of proposed responses.

Joseph Sittler, *Structure of Christian Ethics* (Baton Rouge: Louisiana State University Press, 1958). A stimulating gospel-centered ethic presented in concise form.

Helmut Thielicke, *Theological Ethics,* edited by William H. Lazareth (Philadelphia: Fortress Press, 1966). A Lutheran approach by the great German theologian-preacher. Lucid and relevant even when dealing with profound and ambiguous material.